McCAIN

THE ESSENTIAL GUIDE TO THE REPUBLICAN NOMINEE

His character, his career and where he stands

MARK SILVA

This book is available in quantity at special discounts for your group or organization. For further information, contact:

Triumph Books

542 S. Dearborn Street, suite 750, Chicago, Illinois 60605

Phone 312-939-3339; Fax 312-663-3557

Printed in U.S.A.
ISBN: 978-1-60078-196-4

Cover photo by Chuck Kennedy, McClatchy-Tribune
Back photo by Jay L. Clendenin, Los Angeles Times
Pages 6-7
A crowd at City Hall Plaza in Nashua, N.H., shows its support for Republican presidential nominee John McCain at a January 2008 rally.
Pages 8-9
Sen. John McCain catches up on calls in a Keene, N.H., hotel room in July 2007. "I can out-campaign anyone," he says. "It won't be easy. But it's not supposed to be easy. [The presidency] is the most important job in the world."
Pages 10-11
McCain takes the stage with his wife, Cindy, at the Florida Press Association/Florida Society of Newspaper Editors convention at Disney World in Orlando in June 2008.

"It is easy to forget in politics where principle ends and selfishness begins. It takes leaders of courage and character to remember the difference."

John McCain, address to Republican National Convention, Philadelphia, Aug. 1, 2000

"When I was a young man, I was quite infatuated with self-expression, and rightly so because, if memory conveniently serves, I was so much more eloquent, well-informed and wiser than anyone else I knew."

McCain, commencement address, Liberty University, Lynchburg, Va., May 13, 2006

Contents

McCAIN

LIVE
TUCKER
COMMISSION ON VETERANS' CARE URGES

This book is dedicated to those who have encouraged me most,
my parents, Daniel and Lorraine Silva,
who taught me about work and ethics, my wife, Nina Sichel,
who knows something about writing and rootlessness,
and my children, Lisa and Dylan Silva,
who know how to make a man proud.

Introduction: The Warrior

JOHN MCCAIN struck a familiar, comfortable pose one wintry day in Derry, N.H. Microphone in hand, he stood by a four-legged stool inside one of the intimate and open-ended town hall-style assemblies that he has made the signature of his two campaigns for the White House. It was Jan. 3, 2008, days before the primary election in a state whose notoriously independent-minded voters would rekindle his decade-old hopes of winning the Republican Party's presidential nomination.

McCain confronted a questioner, a man who pointedly noted: "President Bush has talked about our staying in Iraq for 50 years."

"Maybe 100," McCain interrupted.

"Is that ..." the man attempted to ask.

"How long... we've been in South Korea," McCain forcefully explained, halting his questioner again. "We've been in Japan for 60 years, we've been in South Korea for 50 years or so. That'd be fine with me, as long as Americans..."

"So that's your policy?" the man pressed.

"As long as Americans are not being injured or harmed or wounded or killed," McCain said, "then it's fine with me."

McCain's candid thought — that American military forces may have to play some role in Iraq long after they stop suffering casualties there — was swiftly swept away in the tide of a modern media campaign. McCain's characteristically blunt words about an already unpopular war have returned to haunt him in the specter of television ads aired by opponents eager to manipulate one of the central debates of the 2008 contest for the presidency, the future course of a costly, unyielding war: "100 years," his opponents warned, echoing his words, "fine with me."

"This is Alex. He's my first," said the emotional young mother of an infant son seated in her lap for a TV ad aired by MoveOn.org. The anti-war organization was supporting McCain's Democratic rival, Sen. Barack Obama, who has pledged to remove U.S. troops from Iraq within 16 months. "John McCain, when you say you would stay in Iraq for 100 years, were you counting on Alex?" asked the woman, staring defiantly into the TV ad camera's lens. "Because, if you were, you can't have him."

Perhaps this is the price of controversy that any plain-spoken candidate for president must pay. But McCain, more plain-spoken than most, isn't merely direct. He is so adamant that America can and must prevail at war that he has flatly declared: "I'd much rather lose a campaign than lose a war."

McCain's own extraordinary life experiences explain more about the outlook he brings to his campaign for president than any words ever will. John Sidney McCain is a son and grandson of four-star admirals with the same name, veterans of the great world wars. His ancestors on both sides have fought in American conflicts since the Revolutionary War. One served on the staff of George Washington. His father's side fought and died for the Confederacy in the Civil War. And McCain is a scarred and decorated veteran of his own unpopular war. He was held and tortured for 5½ years, two in solitary confinement, as a prisoner of war after the bomber he piloted in Vietnam was shot down by a surface-to-air missile over Hanoi. He broke his arms and leg in the ejection from his airplane and was pulled from a lake and beaten. Raised in "the culture of the Navy" and not rooted in any one place, he is a third-generation graduate of the U.S. Naval Academy, albeit a relentless mischief-maker who finished near the bottom of his class. His son Jack is near graduation from the academy. His younger son Jimmy enlisted in the Marines at 17 and was deployed to Iraq.

"I detest war," McCain said during a speech to the Los Angeles World Affairs Council in March 2008. "I hate war," he has said in his own campaign TV ad countering his opposition. "Only a fool or a fraud talks tough or romantically about war."

"I am an idealist," McCain has said. "I am, from hard experience and the judgment it informs, a realistic idealist."

He is also a joker of the first order. The seriousness of his appeal for support is leavened with a self-effacing humor that first found a national audience in his 2000 campaign for the GOP's presidential nomination — a contest launched with his stunning victory over George W. Bush in New Hampshire but then lost in a bruising, personally bitter primary battle with Bush.

"It doesn't take a lot of talent to be shot down," McCain advised audiences of his own war story during the 2000 contest. "I intercepted a surface-to-air missile with my own airplane."

"I'm older than dirt," he often replies in jest to questions about his age. "And I have more scars than Frankenstein," jokes McCain, who underwent skin

At the airport in Allentown, Pa., John McCain goes from his "Straight Talk Express" plane to his bus in June 2008.

cancer surgery on his face in 2000. He moves somewhat stiffly at times, limited by a shoulder broken at war and in captivity when his arms were tied behind his back as a prisoner of war.

He campaigned as a truth-teller — "I will always tell the truth," he promised in 2000 — a self-styled reformer intent on ridding Washington of the influence of special-interest money. And he spoke from damaging personal experience: Early in his more than 21-year career in the U.S. Senate, the young senator from Arizona became ensnared in a scandal involving Charles Keating, the owner of a failing savings and loan association who called on friends in Congress to exert some pressure on federal banking regulators. McCain, who had collected campaign contributions from Keating and flown on his plane, and four other members of Congress met with the regulators. They became known as the "Keating Five" in a Senate ethics probe that ultimately cleared McCain, but he admitted "poor judgment" in attending the meetings. He emerged from that episode with a determination to limit the money lavished on political parties by wealthy donors, joining Democratic Sen. Russell Feingold of Wisconsin in a years-long campaign to restrain the "soft money" of unfettered political donors that ultimately produced a "McCain-Feingold" bill imposing caps on contributions to political parties and limiting campaign ads that unions and corporations could run. Still, Bush turned McCain's association with lobbyists against him, accusing the chairman of the Senate Commerce Committee of "ringing the iron triangle of money and influence like a dinner bell."

McCain, who had been dubbed a "maverick" by The Washington Post in the early 1990s, also patented a certain campaign style with his "Straight Talk Express." His opened his bus to reporters ready to ride the trail with a senior senator from Arizona who had a penchant for answering questions until no one had any more.

When I first met him aboard a campaign plane then, McCain was asked about his recently released book, "Faith of My Fathers," which detailed not only the history of his fabled military family, but also his own embarrassing exploits as a midshipman who risked expulsion and finished fifth from the bottom of his class at Annapolis. Asked whether he had held back some of his best stories from that campaign-launching book, McCain rolled his eyes, rummaged through a deep catalog of tales and offered one about "borrowing" an airplane from the Navy and buzzing his buddies at Virginia Beach.

Yet, for all his avowed straight talk, McCain engaged in some of his own double-talk in that campaign for which he later, in characteristic candor, apologized. Campaigning in South Carolina, where the Confederate flag still flew from the top of the state Capitol in Columbia and had become a supercharged issue in the state's 2000 primary elections, McCain called the flag "very offensive" to many Americans and "a symbol of racism and slavery." McCain would come to learn that his own great-great grandfather, an officer in the Confederate Army who had owned a plantation in Carroll County, Miss., was a slaveholder. But he would not take a position on flying the flag, instead calling it an issue for the state to settle. Only after he lost South Carolina, and ultimately the party's nomination, to Bush, did McCain return to Columbia in April 2000 to admit that he had not been forthcoming during his campaign. Declaring bluntly that Confederate soldiers had "fought on the wrong side of American history," McCain allowed that his dodge "broke my promise to always tell the truth. ... I feared that if I answered honestly, I could not win the South Carolina primary," he told the South Carolina Policy Council. "So I chose to compromise my principles." On July 1, the flag came down from the top of the Statehouse after 38 years.

McCain, who faced a vicious campaign of underground rumors about himself and his family in that South Carolina contest, ran against Bush with a growing ferocity. Accusing his Republican rival of "character assassination," he advanced into a contest in Michigan, his last stand, declaring: "I'm just like Luke Skywalker trying to get out of the Death Star ... I'm telling you," he told an audience in Saginaw, "they're shooting at me from everywhere. Everybody's against me, but we're gonna kill 'em."

The fact that McCain could eventually reconcile with Bush speaks volumes about the necessities of political compromise. The two made a public show of their unity that summer. And in 2008, after McCain clinched his party's presidential nomination, he flew to Washington for a Rose Garden appearance with the president, who acknowledges that his own low public-approval ratings, a result of increased opposition to the war, may make him unwelcome on the campaign trail. Yet the relationship of these two Republicans has remained rocky, with McCain opposing Bush's first round of tax cuts as too heavily weighted toward the wealthy and criticizing the conduct of the Iraq War in its early stages — with particular criticism for former Defense Secretary Donald Rumsfeld; McCain declared that he had lost faith in him before Rumsfeld finally quit. And McCain, who had suffered permanently disfiguring torture at the hands of his North Vietnamese captors, bucked the Bush White House over its insistence on having unchecked latitude in the interrogation of suspected terrorists. McCain fought for and secured a ban against torture by the military.

Thomas Kean, chairman of the 9/11 Commission investigating government intelligence operations after the terrorist attacks of Sept. 11, 2001, found in McCain a fearless advocate who helped wrest additional money for the investigation when the White House was resisting it. McCain helped the commission press for the President's Daily Briefing that Bush had received and for the president's own testimony, Kean said. He always found that the best way to get results was to make an issue public. And at one point, Kean recalled, when he was pushing then-White House Chief of Staff Andrew Card on an issue, Card asked him on the telephone: "You're not going to get McCain going, are you?"

"In my experience with him," Kean said of McCain, who has acknowledged his own capacity for a hot temper at times, "he got a little mad, but it was always on the right things with the right people. He was never out of control. He had a few choice expletives and said, 'We'll get you what you need.'"

McCain has found his role models in John Sidney McCain Sr., who graduated from Annapolis in 1906 and went on to command aircraft carriers and naval aviation, and in John Sidney McCain Jr., who graduated from Annapolis in 1931 to become a submariner and ultimately commander in chief of Pacific forces for all branches of the military early during his own son's captivity in North Vietnam, which began in 1967. Navy destroyers were named after them. "They were my first heroes," McCain told a Veterans of Foreign Wars assembly in Kansas City in 1995, a line that he has repeated many times in his life and campaigns.

Yet McCain retired as a captain in 1981 after two decades in the Navy, and first ran for Congress the following year, serving two terms in the House before

"It doesn't take a lot of talent to be shot down. I intercepted a surface-to-air missile with my own airplane."

John McCain

his first election to the Senate in 1986.

He had returned from war, and torture, wounded and somewhat estranged from his wife, Carol. Their daughter, Sidney, had been born soon before he left for Vietnam. He had adopted his wife's two sons, Doug and Andrew, from her first marriage. At a Navy function in Hawaii years later, as McCain served as the Navy's liaison to the Senate near the close of his military career, he met the daughter of a wealthy beer distributor from Phoenix and quickly fell in love. He divorced his wife and married Cindy Hensley in 1980. When they met, he was 42 and she was 24. They have had three children together, Meghan, Jack and Jimmy, grown now, and they adopted an orphan from Bangladesh, Bridget, a teenager now. Cindy McCain, independently wealthy as chairwoman of Hensley & Co., one of the nation's top Budweiser distributors, raised the children in Arizona while McCain served for the past 25 years in the House and Senate, and commuted home on weekends. She has described her husband's service as another deployment.

McCain was 30 when he left for Vietnam. A pilot of an A-4 bomber launched from aircraft carriers, he was flying his 23rd mission, a bombing raid on a power plant in Hanoi, when his plane was shot down by a surface-to-air missile in 1967. He was 36 when he returned from Vietnam, released from captivity in 1973.

"War is awful," McCain told the VFW in 1995. "We also share — and this is harder to explain — the survivors' humility. ... Every combat veteran remembers those comrades whose sacrifice was eternal. Their loss taught us everything about tragedy and everything about duty. ... I cannot help but wince a little when heroism is ascribed to me. For I once watched men pay a much higher price for that honor than was asked of me."

McCain now wages what could become his final campaign. Should he win this election, McCain would, at 72, become the oldest American ever elected to a first term as president. In his many years of experience, which he touts as his chief attribute, McCain has attained a view of America's role in the world and a personal conceit of patriotism that drive this bid for the White House.

McCain has always relished and embraced the "underdog" label. At the height of his first campaign for president, he told a hall full of grizzled military veterans in rural Franklin, N.H.: "It's been uphill all the way. It's been the kind of fight we like, really — everything against us." He told them: "Let's go down to the old soldiers' home and blow the cavalry charge again."

Yet then McCain was campaigning as an agent of change. "A great national crusade has begun," he told supporters heading out of Nashua, N.H., with a stunning 19-point victory over Bush in that state's 2000 primary. Celebrating to the accompaniment of a brass band's "Anchors Aweigh," McCain told them: "We have sent a powerful message to Washington that change is coming."

And now, McCain faces a Democratic senator from Illinois many years his junior who is campaigning with the same clarion call for change: Barack Obama, who served not a day in the military, who opposed the U.S.-led invasion of Iraq and has pledged to bring troops home within 16 months as president. McCain emerges from his party's nominating convention with a message that his experience will trump the appeal for change on which Obama has waged his campaign. The senior senator from Arizona told an audience at one of his trademark town halls in New Mexico in summer 2008: "The commander in chief doesn't get a learning curve."

1 McCain's Heroes: "In the culture of the Navy"

JOHN SIDNEY MCCAIN III trod a path cleared for him long before he was born. His calling: The career of his heroes. His father was a submariner, his grandfather a naval aviator. His schooling was their schooling, the U.S. Naval Academy. They went to war. He went to war. Yet he would not follow them all the way to the admiralty of the Navy. He once chafed at authority, fearful of the toll it might take on his individuality. And when the recklessness of his youthful rebellion at the academy and rowdiness in the Navy yielded to the maturity of a bomber pilot training for war, his path led him someplace his heroes had never been: The cement floor of a war prison where he was beaten, confined alone and beaten more. But what precluded McCain from pursuing the highest command of the service that consumed his heroes' lives was not so much the surface-to-air missile that downed his Skyhawk over Hanoi but the permanent injuries he suffered in 5½ years of imprisonment.

McCain was born in the Panama Canal Zone on Aug. 29, 1936. But it was no more home to him or his family than Council Bluffs, Iowa, had been to his father, who was also born to a roving Navy family. McCain's father served as an officer aboard a submarine. Three months after the second child, and first son, of Jack and Roberta McCain was born at Coco Solo submarine base in Panama, Jack McCain was transferred to New London, Conn. The couple had eloped three years earlier and were married at Caesar's Bar in Tijuana, when he was serving as an ensign aboard the USS Oklahoma at Long Beach, Calif., and she was a student at the University of Southern California. Her father had objected to her courtship with a sailor.

At John McCain's christening in the Panama Canal Zone in 1936, with father John Sidney McCain Jr. (left) and grandfather John Sidney McCain.

"The relationship of a sailor and his children is, in large part, a metaphysical one," John McCain wrote in his revealing 1999 memoir, "Faith of My Fathers." "Our family lived on the move, rooted not in a location, but in the culture of the Navy."

Generations of the McCain family had served the Navy through the 20th Century, and before that the Army. John McCain Sr. was first in the family to graduate from the U.S. Naval Academy, in 1906, his brother Bill the last to graduate from West Point. "For two centuries," the 2008 Republican nominee for president has written, "the men of my family were raised to go to war."

And the family's history had followed that of the South. Camp McCain, in Grenada, Miss., was named for his grandfather's uncle, Maj. Gen. Henry Pinckney McCain, who had organized the draft during World War I. His great-grandfather, Hugh McCain, had been the first of a family of Scottish Presbyterians to settle in the South. His grandson, William Alexander McCain, was a Mississippi cavalryman who died during the Civil War. He owned a plantation in Carroll County, Miss., called Waverly, after the Sir Walter Scott novels. He owned 52 slaves, according to county records found by Salon.com during the candidate's first campaign for president in 2000 — a fact, McCain maintained then, that he had not known before. "I knew we fought in the Civil War," he told Salon.com. "But no, I had no idea. ... I guess when you really think about it logically, it shouldn't be a surprise. They had a plantation and they fought in the Civil War."

On McCain Jr.'s mother's side, the Scottish Youngs had arrived in the Colonies in 1646. John Young, a militia captain in the Revolutionary War, served on the staff of Gen. George Washington.

McCain's grandfather, John McCain Sr., was born and raised on the Mississippi plantation. He sailed in the "Great White Fleet" of Theodore Roosevelt aboard the USS Connecticut, escorting convoys during World War I. He commanded the carrier USS Ranger and made rear admiral in 1941. He served a stint in Washington as chief of naval aeronautics and returned to the Pacific in the summer of 1944 as commander of the Second Fast Carrier Force. Awarded the Navy Cross, McCain Sr. attended the signing of the Japanese surrender aboard the USS Missouri in 1945. He had finished his career as a four-star admiral, and died just days after returning home to Coronado, Calif. He was 61.

John Sidney McCain III

John McCain Jr. was born in Iowa, where his mother went into labor during a family visit. He entered the Naval Academy at 16 and graduated in 1931. His son the senator has written that his father, like himself, was a troublemaker at the academy — "his grades were poor, his discipline worse." McCain Jr. graduated 18th from the bottom of his class yet followed his father to the highest ranks of the Navy — the first father and son to become four-star admirals. Denied flight school because of a heart murmur, he trained as a submariner. The family was living in New London when Pearl Harbor was bombed. His son, 5 at the time, seldom saw his father during the next four years. During World War II, John McCain Jr. commanded three subs in the Pacific

John McCain's father and grandfather on the bridge of the USS Proteus on Sept. 2, 1945, in Tokyo Bay shortly after the signing of the Japanese surrender. It was the last time father and son saw each other. The senior McCain, 61, died days after returning home to California.

Vice Adm. John S. McCain Jr. (center) is welcomed aboard the USS DeSoto County by its commander, Lt. Cmdr. H.D. Mann, in August 1964 at Navy Pier in Chicago.

"The commandant was neither the first nor the last person to accuse me of being spoiled, implying that my parents had greased my way in the world."

John McCain

and was awarded the Silver Star and Bronze Star. After service aboard a cruiser in the Korean War, he became the Navy's senior officer liaison to Congress, a post that his son later held at the conclusion of his own naval career. He commanded Amphibious Forces Atlantic and rose to commander in chief, Pacific Command, in 1968, as the Vietnam War reached its height. He attained that command soon after his son, a bomber pilot from the carrier Oriskany, was shot down over Hanoi and taken captive by the North Vietnamese. Adm. McCain served as CINCPAC through much of his son's imprisonment, which the younger McCain credits with saving him from the worst torture. In 1972, as the war was winding down, the admiral sought another year in the Pacific but was replaced and retired.

The first of two naval destroyers named for the admirals, the USS John S. McCain, had been commissioned in 1953. It was sold for scrap in late 1979. In 1994, the second, the guided missile destroyer USS John S. McCain, was commissioned. President George H.W. Bush spoke at the christening. The son and grandson of the ship's namesakes, now a senator, attended with his wife.

The senator recalled, in his memoir, the christening of the first ship. He was 17. The legendary Adm. William F. Halsey, who graduated from the Naval Academy two years before McCain's now-deceased grandfather, asked the teenager at the ceremony: "Do you drink, boy?" McCain had "certainly experienced" his share, he recalls, but his mother was with him so he declined the invitation. The admiral insisted, explaining that his grandfather drank bourbon and water. They toasted his grandfather.

McCain doesn't publicly mention his grandfather on his mother's side as much. Archibald Wright had moved from Mississippi to Oklahoma around the turn of the century. He found his fortune in liquor bootlegging, gambling and oil wildcatting in Indian country before settling in Los Angeles. In Muskogee, Okla., he had "stood out in a town full of rascals," a historian at the local library told The Washington Post, citing Oklahoma newspaper accounts from 1908 noting that Arch Wright and an associate had been jailed for 30 days for running gambling at the Mistletoe Bar. Wright plowed his savings into the purchase of a hardware company in Muskogee. And his daughter, Roberta, was born there, in February 1912. Her father died in 1971. But Roberta McCain, at age 96, was still alive to campaign for her son in 2008.

McCain writes of his father's penchant for drink, an "appetite" that grew to overindulgence after his final war. His father returned to Washington in retirement and died of a heart attack in March 1981, a little less than two years before his son was seated in Congress for the first time. He was 70.

If his father had a rebellious streak in his youth, his son inherited it. McCain has written of a dramatic temper as a child, of holding his breath as a 2-year-old until he blacked out. On a doctor's advice, his mother took to dropping him into a tub of cold water fully dressed. In her words, he was "a hell-raiser." He also was shipped from school to school as his family moved around. He learned to assert himself and overcome his slight stature, he has written, by picking a fight with anyone who provoked him. Not until he was 15 did he settle at one boarding school, Episcopal High School in Alexandria, Va., which had a tradition of shipping its own graduates to either the military academies or the Ivy League. He became a wrestler and a football and tennis player. And he was known as a scrapper with the mouth of a sailor.

"He was known as Punk, alternately as Nasty, in another variation, McNasty," wrote Robert Timberg, author of "The Nightingale's Song," which follows the career paths of several wildly different characters who had the Naval Academy in common.

"A rebel without a cause is just a punk," McCain has written in another memoir, "Worth the Fighting For." And he has told many audiences, in person and in print, through the years that he long believed that all glory was "self-glory" — until he found a greater glory in his commitment to his fellow American comrades in the war prisons of Hanoi. He recalls the hazings that freshmen received at Episcopal, much like the hazings that would follow at the academy, and he recalls slipping out at night for bus rides to "burlesque houses" in downtown Washington.

In his senior yearbook, he wrote: "It was three fateful years ago that the 'Punk' first crossed the threshold of The High School. In his time he has become

"A change, subtle at first, came over McCain during a series of deployments to the Mediterranean between 1960 and 1964. To the unpracticed eye, it looked suspiciously like maturity. ... He liked flying off a carrier, enjoyed being at sea and seemed to flourish when assigned additional duties."

Author Robert Timberg

infamous as one of our top-flight wrestlers, lettering for two seasons. His magnetic personality has won for him many life-long friends. But, as magnets must also repel, some have found him hard to get along with. John is remarkable for the amount of gray hair he has; this may come from his cramming for Annapolis or from his nocturnal perambulations. The Naval Academy is his future abode — we hope he will prosper there."

At the academy, as McCain told it years later in "Faith of My Fathers," he "embarked on a four-year course of insubordination and rebellion." As he put it: "Mainly we drank a lot of beer... got in fights." And with a curriculum heavy on math and science, "I got by, just barely at the time, but I got by." He only narrowly avoided expulsion during his final year, as he tells it, and suggests that this was one of those times when his family's legacy had saved him, though his father was just a captain at the time: "The commandant was neither the first nor the last person to accuse me of being spoiled, implying that my parents had greased my way in the world." He ran with a crowd known as "the Bad Bunch."

"THE ONE WITH THE HORNS"

The class of 1,200 that entered the academy in 1954 was whittled down to 899 at the end. At the top of the graduating class: John Poindexter, later to gain some infamy as national security adviser for President Ronald Reagan during the Iran-contra scandal. Poindexter wore the six stripes of a brigade commander at his graduation. Near the bottom: McCain, without a stripe.

Class standing involved more than grades. It also factored in "grease points" for conduct, as Timberg has noted in his book. And McCain had racked up an "astonishing" number of demerits, always just below the threshold for dismissal.

"John Poindexter was the sort of guy with a halo around his head," Annapolis classmate Bill Hemingway was quoted as saying in Timberg's account. "McCain was the one with the horns."

Calling his early Navy days "an even more colorful extension of my rowdy days at the academy," McCain remembers driving a Corvette, dating a lot and spending all his free hours at bars and beach parties. In Pensacola, where he trained to fly in the summer of 1958, the downtown hotspot was a dark bar that served as a magnet for sailors and strippers, Trader John's. McCain dated a girl who worked there known as "Marie, the Flame of Florida," who cleaned her nails with a switchblade.

One night at the Officers' Club, as Timberg tells it, a superior officer called McCain out for his sloppy attire, a torn sweater and cowboy boots, on the shuffleboard court. "A cigarette dangled from his lips," Timberg wrote. The officer asked McCain: "What do you think your grandfather would say?" McCain replied: "Frankly, Commander, I don't think he'd give a rat's ass."

In the early 1960s, McCain flew Douglas A-1 Skyraiders, single-seat, propeller-driven dive torpedo bombers that had been designed near the end of World War II for aircraft-carrier deployment but were launched too late for that war. They had become the staple of carrier forces during the Korean War and were flown into the early stages of the war in Vietnam. Deployed out of Norfolk, McCain sailed on and flew from the USS Intrepid and USS Enterprise, and lived in a house on Virginia Beach known for its revelry. He buzzed that beach with a "borrowed" airplane.

McCain rode out the Cuban Missile Crisis aboard the Enterprise, which sailed toward Cuba as President John Kennedy stared down the Soviets over missiles deployed there. War may have been avoided there, but another one was stirring in Vietnam, and McCain viewed the aerial battlefield as an opportunity.

"A change, subtle at first, came over McCain during a series of deployments to the Mediterranean between 1960 and 1964," Timberg wrote. "To the unpracticed eye, it looked suspiciously like maturity. ... He liked flying off a carrier, enjoyed being at sea and seemed to

John McCain (front right) with his squadron in 1965. Two years later, he would be captured in Vietnam.

DANGER
RUN
WITH

Sailors battle a raging blaze on the deck of the USS Forrestal on July 29, 1967, in the South China Sea 60 miles from North Vietnam. John McCain III's Skyhawk was struck by an accidentally discharged missile, which started a fire that killed 134.

"I didn't realize it at the moment, but I had broken my right leg around the knee, my right arm in three places, and my left arm. I regained consciousness just before I landed by parachute in a lake right in the corner of Hanoi."

John McCain

flourish when assigned additional duties."

"The Navy, especially with a war on, offered the quickest route to adventure if I could manage to avoid committing some career-ending mistake," McCain has written. He aspired to advancement in the Navy but feared that his "reputation for foolishness" would stand in the way of any career in the mold of his forebears.

War, as he tells it, became his road to redemption: "I wanted to go to Vietnam, and to keep faith with the family creed." Again he has told of family influence greasing his path, this time a path to war, with the undersecretary of the Navy helping him get a ticket to Vietnam. He moved to McCain Field in Meridian, Miss., to work on his flying and, by his own account, party harder.

It was during his training at McCain Field that he started dating Carol Shepp, a young model from Philadelphia who had been the wife of a friend and fellow flier he had known since the academy. A friend of McCain's at Annapolis, Alasdair Swanson, had married Carol Shepp in 1958, the year the men graduated. And in the early 1960s, they were living in Pensacola, where McCain and Swanson were flying. The marriage ended in 1964, when Carol claimed infidelity in her divorce suit. McCain started dating her soon afterward. He would fly a Skyraider from Mississippi to Philadelphia to see her on weekends, stopping in Norfolk for fuel, and they married in her hometown on July 3, 1965. McCain adopted her two boys, Doug, then 5, and Andy, then 3. And in September 1966 a girl was born — Sidney, bearing the middle names of her father, grandfather and great-grandfather.

Toward the end of 1966, McCain and his family moved to Jacksonville for his deployment with a squadron aboard the USS Forrestal. He had trained in Mississippi on Douglas A-4 Skyhawks — jet-powered replacements for the A-1s that McCain had flown. The delta-winged "Bantam Bomber" carried two 20 mm cannons and an arsenal of bombs, rockets and missiles on its belly. In 1967, McCain sailed with the Forrestal to Yankee Station, 60 miles from North Vietnam in the South China Sea.

On July 29, 1967, Lt. Cmdr. McCain already had flown five bombing runs over North Vietnam when his Skyhawk stood third in line on the port side of the Forrestal. The Skyhawks were carrying 500- and 1,000-pound bombs, and to extend their range their bellies were fitted with two 200-gallon fuel tanks. The day was "as typical as it could be ... for men at war," according to an account from Naval Aviation News that year. The 80,000-ton ship carried 5,000 officers and enlisted men. From the waters of the Gulf of Tonkin, they were launching strikes against a coastline just over the horizon. For four days, Attack Carrier Air Wing 17 had flown 150 missions against targets in North Vietnam. A hot, tropical sun cooked the deck of the carrier shortly before noon. A Zuni missile accidentally discharged in the startup of one of the F-4 Phantom fighter jets that would fly cover for the bomb raid. It struck one of McCain's fuel tanks and started a fire that quickly engulfed several bombers in flaming jet fuel. McCain escaped through billowing black smoke and recalls rolling through flames, his flight suit catching fire. As he started toward another pilot attempting to escape from his cockpit, an explosion blew him backward, lodging shrapnel in his thighs and chest. Before it was contained, the Forrestal fire killed 134 aboard and injured 62. Fires persisted for another day below deck after the casualty-strewn flight deck was cleared.

The Forrestal was pulled out of service for repair in the Philippines, and McCain moved to the USS Oriskany at the end of September to fly with a Skyhawk squadron known as the Saints. In three years of Operation Rolling Thunder, concluding in 1968, 38 pilots from the Oriskany were killed or captured. The Oriskany also had suffered an accidental fire that killed 44 aboard in 1966.

McCain confided in a friend, Chuck Larson, an academy classmate and fellow flier in training at Pensacola who went on to become an admiral and commander in chief of Pacific forces, that he was worried about his naval career. Everywhere he went, he told Larson, his reputation preceded him. "I'm serious about the Navy," McCain told Larson. "If I can't get people to take me seriously, maybe I'll have to try something else."

McCain, who had survived 22 bomb runs over North Vietnam when he launched from the Oriskany on Oct. 26, 1967, recalls the criticism he and fellow fliers had for the "senseless" tactics and Washington-dictated, often-repeating targets of Rolling Thunder: "In all candor, we thought our civilian commanders were complete idiots who didn't have the least notion of what it took to win the war," he wrote in "Faith of My Fathers."

A FATEFUL MISSION
But for McCain, any such consideration of air tactics ended on this, his 23rd bomb run, an attack on a power plant in Hanoi. As McCain was leaving the ready room, an officer warned him to be careful: "We're probably going to lose someone on this one."

Hanoi's defenses stood ready for the attack. On the approach to Hanoi, the lights in McCain's Skyhawk alerted him that he was a locked target. McCain ruefully recalls the image of a surface-to-air missile appearing as "a flying telephone pole." In the flak-filled sky over Hanoi, a SAM tore the right wing off his bomber.

"I pulled the ejection handle and was knocked unconscious by the force of the ejection," McCain wrote in an account for U.S. News and World Report in 1973, the year he returned home. "I didn't realize it at the moment, but I had broken my right leg around the knee, my right arm in three places, and my left arm. I regained consciousness just before I landed by parachute in a lake right in the corner of Hanoi." As a crowd pulled the downed American from Truc Bach Lake in Hanoi, McCain was beaten by a crowd and his shoulder broken with a rifle butt. He also recalls a woman who intervened in the beating, offered him tea and applied bamboo splints to his breaks as a crowd of hundreds retreated. He had fallen not far from the legendary French-built prison Hoa Lo, which prisoners of war dubbed "Hanoi Hilton."

On Oct. 26, 1967, Navy fighter pilot John McCain (center) is captured by Vietnamese civilians in Truc Bach Lake in Hanoi.

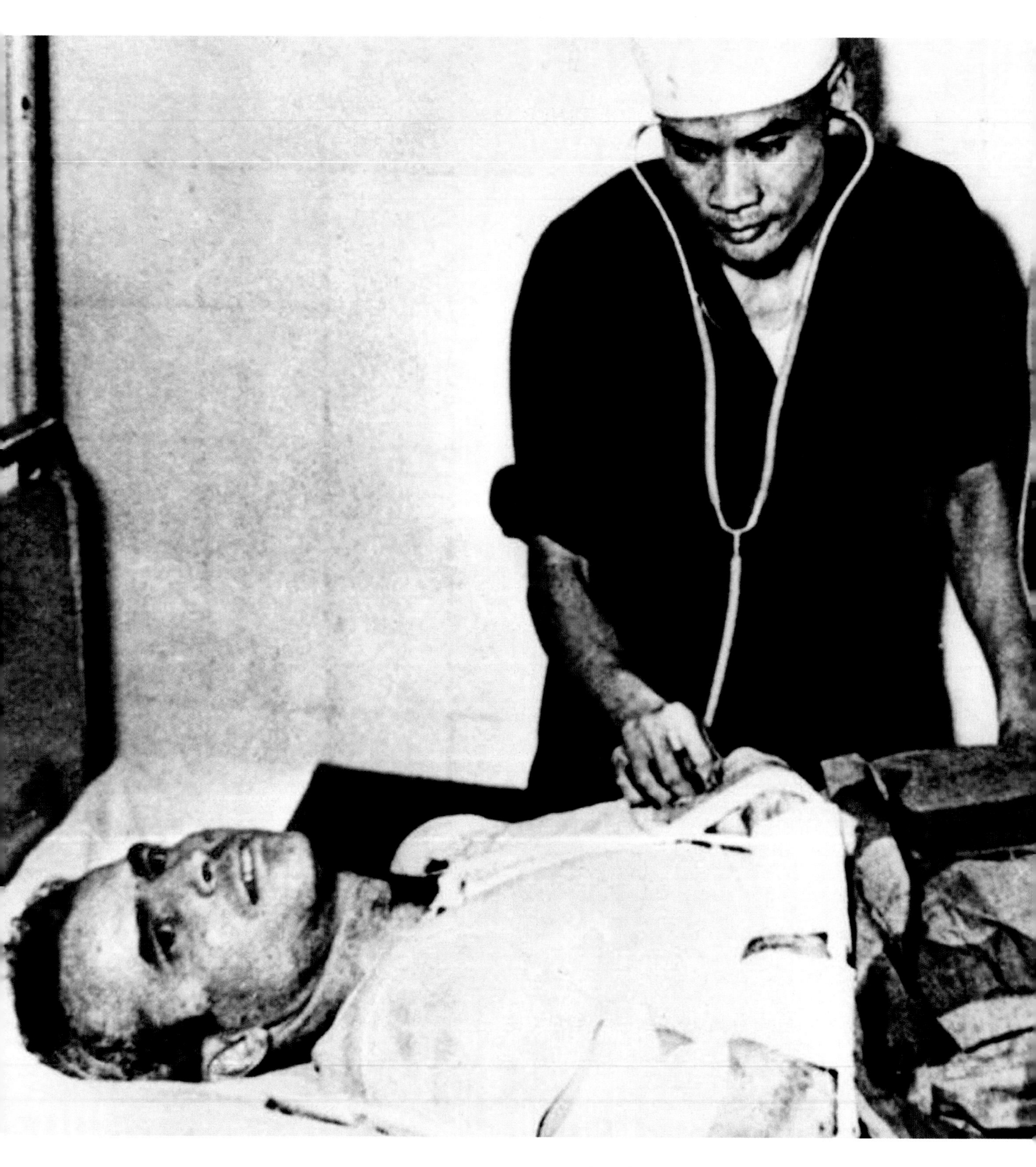

A photo from the North Vietnamese government shows John McCain in a Hanoi hospital as a prisoner of war in fall 1967.

2 *Prisoner of War: "He chose honor"*

LT. CMDR. JOHN MCCAIN did not suffer the worst of the torture meted out to prisoners of war in Hanoi. He did suffer abuse that, to this day, limits the reach of his shoulders. In 5½ years of imprisonment, interrogations and beatings at the war prison famously known as "Hanoi Hilton," at "The Plantation" and at "Camp Unity" — including two years of solitary confinement in a 10-by-10-foot cell with a dim light bulb never extinguished — he learned more about himself than the Naval Academy had ever taught him. Early in his captivity, he did succumb to forcible demands for a confession, which really was no confession at all but exceeded the bounds of name, rank and serial number. When pressed to name pilots in the attack force based at his aircraft carrier at sea, he would offer up the names of the front line of the Green Bay Packers. Early in his confinement, he refused an offer for release, abiding by a Code of Conduct that dictated that prisoners of war captured first must be released first. He did benefit from a certain special treatment that stemmed from the advantage that the North Vietnamese had shot down the son of an admiral. McCain's father was commander of naval forces in Europe. And, on the first American Independence Day of McCain's captivity in Hanoi, in July 1968, unbeknownst to the prisoner of war at the time, his father became commander in chief of Pacific forces, overseer of the U.S. war in Vietnam. The North Vietnamese, as one of their harsher prison officers informed a fellow prisoner of McCain's, had captured "the Crown Prince."

Through the years, McCain has recounted not only torture, but also kindness at the hands of his captors: The guard who came in to loosen the ropes that bound the prisoner's arms, pulled so far behind his back that they forced already damaged shoulders into painful positions, with the guard later returning to tighten the ropes at the end of his shift. Or the guard who traced an image of the cross in the sand before him on Christmas Day, then brushed it away as he left. And he has spoken of the camaraderie of captives, who taught him a sense of duty to others that he had never fully known.

Through the years, McCain has repeated tales of inspiration he encountered in captivity: Most often the heroism of fellow captive Mike Christian, who had sewn a small American flag inside his shirt with a bamboo needle. Each night before a supper of soup, as McCain has recounted many times in public since then, the prisoners would take out the flag and say the Pledge of Allegiance. When guards confiscated Christian's flag and hauled him outside for a beating, cell mates cleaned him up and settled him to rest — then watched as he pulled out a bamboo needle, with eyes nearly swollen shut, and started sewing anew.

The years of captivity became, at the time, the longest McCain had ever known in one place.

Taken after his capture to the "Hanoi Hilton," McCain, 31, was laid on a stretcher on the floor of a cell, his fractured leg grossly swollen, and told he would see no medical care until he volunteered some useful information. For a few days, he passed in and out of consciousness, offering only name, rank and serial number and getting kicked and punched for his refusal to cooperate. McCain has written that, after days of interrogation, he finally gave his captors the name of his carrier, the Oriskany, and his squadron number and confirmed that his target had been the power plant. Beaten for more, he gave them Packers' names. It was innocuous information, but he has conceded with some embarrassment that it exceeded the Code of Conduct for American POWs.

As his leg worsened, he conjured up the image of a fellow pilot who had suffered a similar injury, gone into shock and died. He asked for medical treatment. The camp doctor arrived, took his pulse and whispered to an interpreter, who said: "It's too late."

Hours later, an interrogator arrived and told McCain: "Your father is a big admiral. Now we take you to the hospital."

The hospital was little better. After two weeks, a doctor attempted to set multiple breaks in McCain's right arm, working without painkillers as he manipulated the bones and failing with attempts so painful that the screaming prisoner passed out. The doctor gave up and wrapped McCain in a cast from neck to waist.

His cast still drying, McCain was moved to another room, where a French television crew was waiting. He insisted that he didn't want to be filmed but was told he needed operations for his injuries and would never get that help if he didn't cooperate. In the film, broadcast by CBS News, McCain told his wife, Carol, and his children that he loved them but refused to mouth the words that his captors were seeking — that he was being treated well and wanted to see the war end swiftly. The French TV correspondent, Francois Chalais, asked McCain how the food in prison was. "Well," McCain replied, "It's OK, but it's not Paris."

He never saw a bath or razor during six weeks in that hospital, but he did get one rudimentary operation for his knee, which never fully recovered. And they never attempted to reset his broken left arm. He was moved to a prison camp known as "The Plantation," housed in a cell with two other officers. One of them, who helped nurse McCain, accepted an early release. The second was moved out of the cell. And for the next two years plus, McCain held a cell by himself.

"My room was fairly decent-sized — I'd say it was about 10 by 10," he wrote for U.S. News & World Report after returning home from Vietnam. "The door was solid. There were no windows. The only ventilation came from two small holes at the top in the ceiling, about 6 inches by 4 inches. The roof was tin, and it got hot as hell in there. The room was kind of dim — night and day — but they always kept on a small light bulb so they could observe me." McCain and the other isolated American prisoners started communicating with taps on the walls.

"IT'S AN AWFUL THING, SOLITARY"

"As far as this business of solitary confinement goes — the most important thing for survival is communication with someone, even if it's only a wave or a wink, a tap on the wall, or to have a guy put his thumb up. It makes all the difference," he wrote in May 1973. "Some guys were interested in mathematics, so they worked out complex formulas in their heads — we were never allowed to have writing materials. Others would build a whole house, from basement on up. I have more of a philosophical bent. I had read a lot of history. I spent days on end going back over those history books in my mind, figuring out where this country or that country went wrong, what the U.S. should do in the area of foreign affairs. I thought a lot about the meaning of life.

"It was easy to lapse into fantasies," he wrote. "I used to write books and plays in my mind, but I doubt that any of them would have been above the level of the cheapest dime novel."

"It's an awful thing, solitary," McCain later wrote in

Lt. Cmdr. John McCain III, a POW for 5½ years, arrives in Jacksonville on March 18, 1973. At left is his wife, Carol, and son Doug, on crutches after breaking a leg in a soccer game.

his 1999 memoir, "Faith of My Fathers." "It crushes your spirit and weakens your resistance... Solitary put me in a pretty surly mood, and I would resist depression by hollering insults at my guards, resorting to the belligerence that I had relied on earlier in my life."

In June 1968, after eight months of captivity, McCain was offered release. He knew the reason: his father's admiralty. He also knew the POW's code: First imprisoned, first released. After days of entreaties to accept the offer, he was asked for his "final answer" on the 4th of July. His answer was no. That day, his father had become CINCPAC, a fact McCain would not learn for another year, from another downed pilot. As he recalled in his memoir, he was told that day: "Now it will be very bad for you."

McCain has recalled the treatment of one particularly "sadistic" interrogator who would order him tied up and left for the night, his biceps bound hard to cut off

circulation and the rope pulled behind his back, yanking his elbows and shoulders. "It was incredibly painful," he has written, yet they allowed the sleeves of his prison shirt to pad the ropes around his biceps, and he was never placed in ankle stocks or leg irons as others were. He was also never whipped with fan belts and never beaten to near-death.

He suffered some "very severe treatment" for about a year and a half, he wrote in 1973. He recalled one beating suffered after he insulted a guard — the prisoner called the keeper an "animal."

"When I said that, the guards, who were all in the room — about 10 of them — really laid into me," he wrote for U.S. News & World Report. "They bounced me from pillar to post, kicking and laughing and scratching. After a few hours of that, ropes were put on me and I sat that night bound with ropes. Then I was taken to a small room. For punishment they would almost always take you to another room where you didn't have a mosquito net or a bed or any clothes. For the next four days, I was beaten every two to three hours by different guards. My left arm was broken again and my ribs were cracked." After four days, he finally succumbed to their demands that he sign a false confession: As a "black criminal" and "air pirate," he had bombed a school.

"Many guys broke at one time or another," McCain wrote in "Faith of My Fathers." "I doubt anyone gets over it entirely. ... I can summon up its feeling in an instant whenever I let myself remember the day."

He has also recalled the humanity of some of his captors. One day, when he had been tied for hours, his arms fastened behind his back and the rope pulled over his head tucked between his legs, a guard entered and "put his finger to his lips, and he loosened the ropes that held me," McCain told an audience in Washington in 2007, repeating a tale that he has told many times. "About five hours later, ... he came back, tightened the ropes and left." Then, on Christmas Day, "who comes walking up ... but the gun guard. ... With his sandal, he drew a cross on the ground and he stood there. And then shortly thereafter he, with his sandal, rubbed out the cross and walked away."

McCain was eventually allowed to write one letter home monthly, and his wife, Carol, would write monthly — though the letters or their contents were often withheld from him. He was allowed one short-sleeve shirt, one long-sleeve, one pair of pants, one pair of rubber sandals, a drinking cup, teapot, toothbrush, toothpaste, bar of soap and one small cloth as a towel. He was allotted three cigarettes a day, which were sometimes denied as punishment.

Toward the end of 1969, the torture ended and the North Vietnamese had started freeing sick or injured prisoners. By the end of the year, McCain was returned to Hoa Lo, the so-called Hilton, and in March 1970 his solitary confinement ended.

By Christmas 1970, McCain and many others were transferred to "Camp Unity," which contained several large cell blocks with a few dozen prisoners in each block.

Orson Swindle, a Marine captain from Camilla, Ga., whose F-8 Crusader had been shot down near the Demilitarized Zone of Vietnam on Nov. 11, 1966 — nearly a year before McCain was captured — was already a prisoner at Camp Unity. Although they were held next-door to each other and communicated with the foot-tapping code of the POWs, they did not meet face-to-face until the spring of 1971, according to Swindle. "He was, by and large, of good spirits, trying to help others maintain their spirits ... one of the most intelligent fellows I've ever met, fiercely loyal to us as prisoners of war," said Swindle, who had suffered his own severe torture, including more than a week chained to a stool and deprived of sleep, and had a reputation as a hard one to break. McCain "obviously had been through a lot and had survived — a tough guy," Swindle said. "He cared deeply about and respected those who were imprisoned with him. As he has often said, he had the privilege of serving among heroes. He learned, as we all did, that you weren't going to survive this by serving yourself."

"TO LIVE OR POSSIBLY DIE"

McCain also had been offered something that few prisoners of war were: early release. But the admiral's son had refused it. "He faced, literally, life and death," Swindle said of his fellow POW in an interview for this book. "He had to make a choice to live or possibly die, and he chose honor. He knew that if he accepted early release, it would be such a propaganda coup that his code of honor and sense of duty would not let that happen. I don't know that we teach that anymore. He said, 'I may die, but I'm damn sure not going to die in a dishonorable fashion.'"

Toward the end of 1972, as McCain recalls it, he and fellow POWs rejoiced when the bombing of Hanoi resumed — a mammoth B-52 campaign approved by President Richard Nixon but launched under the orders of a long-held POW's father — Adm. Jack McCain.

Adm. John McCain Jr. and his son Lt. Cmdr. John McCain on March 31, 1973, in Jacksonville, seeing each other for the first time since the younger McCain returned from a North Vietnamese prison. Adm. McCain was chief of U.S. forces in the Pacific during part of the time his son was imprisoned.

"I had read a lot of history. I spent days on end going back over those history books in my mind, figuring out where this country or that country went wrong, what the U.S. should do in the area of foreign affairs. I thought a lot about the meaning of life."

John McCain

Within weeks, talks for a peace accord were under way. And on Jan. 27, 1973, the accord was signed. McCain was returned to "The Plantation," where the guards had become friendly and prisoners of war were playing bridge.

By March, McCain's name appeared on a prison roster for release. He and others were transported by truck to Gia Lam Airport in Hanoi, where a C-141 transport was waiting to fly them to the Philippines. McCain had been given new crutches but recalls walking to the plane without them. On March 14, 1973, he stepped out at Clark Air Base and was greeted at the ramp by Adm. Noel Gayler, who had replaced his father as CINCPAC.

McCain was 36 years old.

"Now that I'm back, I find a lot of hand-wringing about this country," McCain wrote in the 13-page article for U.S. News & World Report two months later. "I don't buy that. I think America today is a better country than the old I left nearly six years ago. ... I had a lot of time to think over there and came to the conclusion that one of the most important things in life — along with a man's family — is to make some contribution to his country."

That May, Nixon received McCain and others at a White House reception for former POWs. The white-haired lieutenant commander in white dress uniform and decorations leaned into his crutches as he gripped the president's hand with his right hand. As McCain tells it, he had learned something about glory along the way to his release from a prisoner-of-war camp.

"When I was a young man, I thought glory was the highest ambition and all glory was self-glory," McCain told an audience of conservative Republicans in Washington in 2007. He learned, he said, that "I had to have faith in something greater than myself, not only to survive, but to survive with my self-respect intact."

McCain, who has written memoirs with the assistance of a longtime Senate chief of staff and speechwriter, Mark Salter, has a way of returning to his own words time and again, in campaign speeches, in writing and in addresses to audiences. It's as if the words, carefully crafted, contain some comfort of their own.

"We do share a secret," McCain told an audience of veterans in Kansas City in March 1995, some 22 years after his release as a prisoner of war, "but it is not a romantic remembrance of war. War is awful. When nations seek to resolve their differences by force of arms, a million tragedies ensue. Nothing, not the valor with which it is fought, nor the nobility of the cause it serves, can glorify war. War is wretched beyond description ..."

"Only a fool or a fraud sentimentalizes the cruel and merciless reality of war," McCain said, with words that reappeared in 2008 in his election campaign commercials.

"We also share — and this is harder to explain — the survivor's humility," McCain told his fellow veterans of war. "I am not talking about shame. I know of no shame in surviving combat. But every combat veteran remembers those comrades whose sacrifice was eternal. Their loss taught us everything about tragedy and everything about duty ...

"I suspect that at one time or another almost everyone in this room has been called a hero," he said. "I cannot help but wince a little when heroism is ascribed to me. For I once watched men pay a much higher price for that honor than was asked of me. The memory of them, of what they bore for country and honor, helped me to see the virtue in my own humility," McCain said. "It is in that humility, and only in that humility, that the memory of almost all human experiences — love and hate, loss and redemption, joy and despair, suffering and release, regret and gratitude — resides."

President Richard Nixon greets Lt. Cmdr. McCain during a reception for former prisoners of war in May 1973 in Washington, D.C.

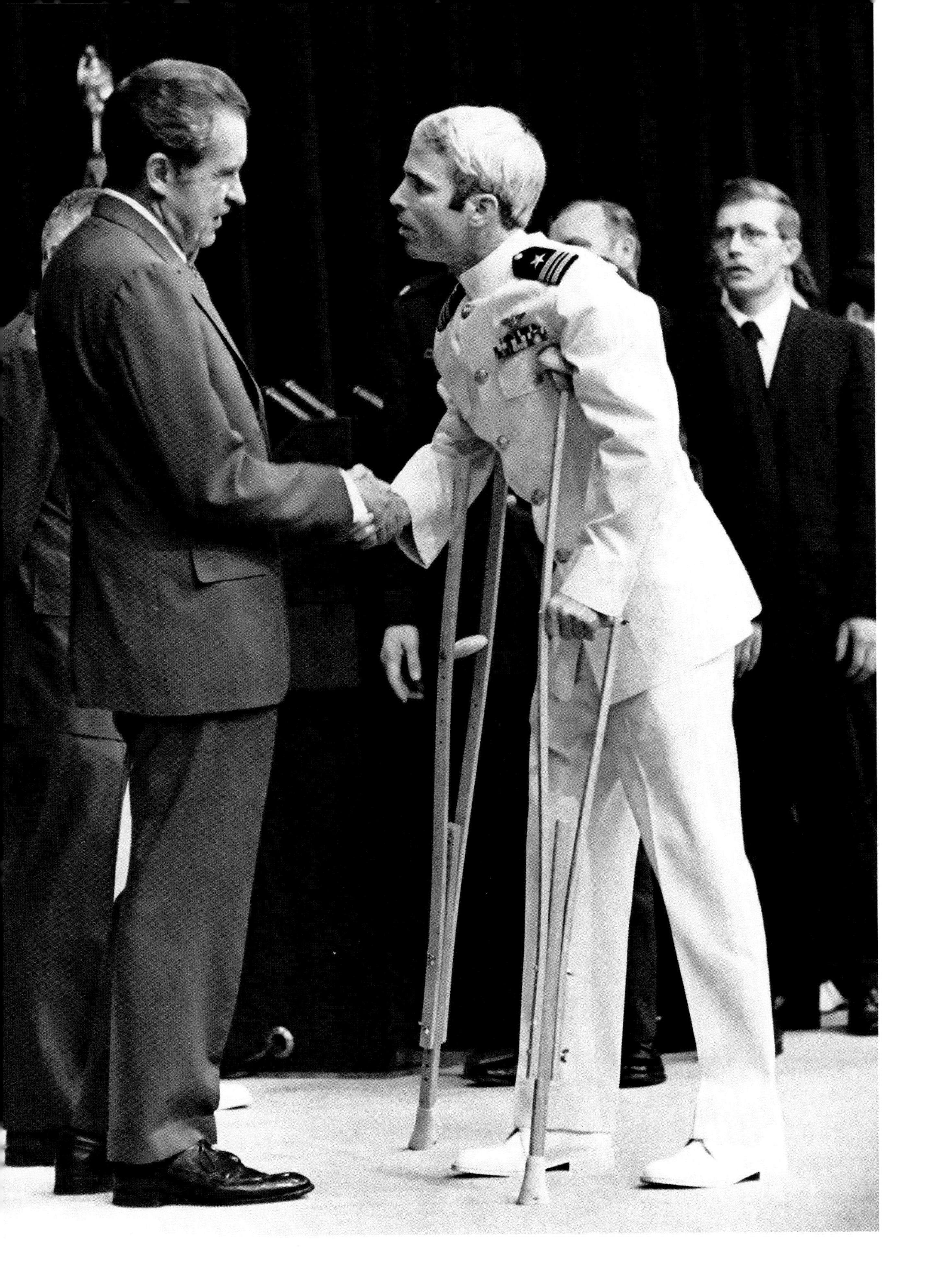

3 *His Second Life: "Everybody's sort of dazzled"*

IN 1982, a year after he retired from the Navy as a captain, and two years after he married the daughter of a wealthy Budweiser distributor in Phoenix, John McCain was waging his first campaign for Congress. Critics were calling him a carpetbagger.

"Listen, pal," McCain snapped at one such questioner during an Arizona candidate forum that year. "I spent 22 years in the Navy. My grandfather was in the Navy. We in the military service tend to move a lot. We have to live in all parts of the country, all parts of the world. I wish I could have had the luxury, like you, of growing up and living and spending my entire life in a nice place like the 1st District of Arizona, but I was doing other things.

"As a matter of fact," McCain added, "when I think about it now, the place I lived longest in my life was Hanoi."

In his second life, McCain had settled into a new home with the help of his wealthy wife, who bought a house in the district where McCain wanted to run. In the year between retirement from the Navy and his first bid for Congress, he had worked in public relations for the Hensley family beer distributorship — a cause that, one executive has noted, really needed no public relations.

John McCain and Cindy Hensley had married on May 17, 1980, a little over a year after meeting in Hawaii, where her father, a bombardier in World War II, had taken her to a Navy reception and she met McCain, the famed POW serving as the Navy's liaison to the Senate. McCain maintains that he was already separated from his wife Carol when he started dating Cindy Hensley. But he did not sue his first wife for divorce until Feb. 19, 1980, and wrote in his petition that he and his wife had "cohabited" until Jan. 7 of that year — nine months after he had first met Hensley.

His first wife, Carol, had a terrible car accident while he was imprisoned in Hanoi. The surgery left her 4 inches shorter. In correspondence with her at the time, he offered some consoling words: He wasn't in much better shape himself.

A few days after landing at Clark Air Base after his release from Hanoi, McCain flew to Jacksonville. His wife and children had spent much of their time in Orange Park awaiting his release. Robert Timberg, author of "The Nightingale's Song," has written of Carol's hopes for the long-delayed reunion: "I thought, of course, we would live happily ever after."

They bought a small cinderblock bungalow by the beach, her dream home. McCain could have been facing retirement from the Navy for medical reasons, with a knee he could barely bend. Doctors in Jacksonville said there was little they could do, that too much time had passed. McCain wanted to fly again, and he found his answer in a physical therapist who called on him when he went up to Ft. McNair in Washington, D.C., as a student at the National War College that summer. By summer's end, after a lot of painful therapy, he had regained much of the range in his knee and went to Pensacola for medical testing. He was cleared to fly — though he joked that he probably wouldn't be able to extend his arm high enough if he ever needed to throw an ejection switch again.

The McCains also had struck up a relationship with Ronald and Nancy Reagan. In spring 1973, they went to

In the Oval Office, President Ronald Reagan speaks with Rep. John McCain of Arizona, a candidate for Senate, in 1986.

"The breakup of our marriage was not caused by my accident or Vietnam or any of those things. ... I attribute it more to John turning 40 and wanting to be 25 again more than I do anything else."

John McCain's first wife, Carol

Los Angeles, where McCain would testify against Daniel Ellsberg, who had leaked the Pentagon Papers to the press. McCain, a well-known former POW now, was ready to speak to the harm that Americans could have suffered with the release of those papers. But the case against Ellsberg was dismissed. And the McCains traveled to San Francisco, where Ross Perot was hosting a homecoming for POWs at the Fairmont Hotel. John was on crutches. Carol had crutches and a wheelchair. Nancy Reynolds, an assistant to Gov. Reagan at the time, told Timberg that McCain arrived with the mien of a natural celebrity: "He walks into a room and it's bing, bing, bing, and everybody's sort of dazzled." She arranged for a meeting between the McCains and the Reagans, and the governor played host to the famous former POW and his wife at his home in Pacific Palisades.

The following year, his last as governor, Reagan invited McCain to speak at a prayer breakfast in Sacramento. "Nancy cries when we send out the laundry," Reagan told the audience, "so I want to tell you, she'll never make it through listening to a talk by our next guest, Cmdr. John McCain."

"A SERIES OF DALLIANCES"

McCain found his wings again, returning to Jacksonville in 1974 as executive officer of Replacement Air Group 174 and a few months later becoming its commander. But in Jacksonville, wrote Timberg, McCain "started carousing and running around with women. ... He admitted to having a series of dalliances during this period" but denied rumors that they involved subordinates in his command. McCain and his wife had become increasingly estranged since his return from war.

"I had changed, she had changed," McCain told the author. "People who have been apart that much change." Carol was more blunt about her former husband, telling Timberg: "The breakup of our marriage was not caused by my accident or Vietnam or any of those things. ... I attribute it more to John turning 40 and wanting to be 25 again more than I do anything else."

In his autobiographical "Worth the Fighting For," McCain maintained that "my marriage's collapse was attributable to my own selfishness and immaturity. The blame was entirely mine."

In spring 1979, a young and beautiful Cindy Lou Hensley joined her parents on a trip to Hawaii. At a cocktail party in Honolulu, McCain, the Navy's chief liaison to the Senate en route to Asia, walked over to introduce himself. "He was [42], but told her he was 37," Newsweek has reported. "Cindy was 24, but told him she was 27. By both accounts, it was love at first sight."

For the next few months, McCain and Hensley traveled between Washington and Arizona to see each other. He proposed at the Capitol. In February 1980, he filed for divorce. In April, the marriage was dissolved, and in May, McCain and Hensley married at the Arizona Biltmore.

Carol McCain found work with a family friend, serving as a personal aide to Nancy Reagan during the 1980 presidential campaign, and then running the White House Visitors Office. She later worked in press relations in the Washington area and retired from the National Soft Drink Association. Her son Andy is a vice president with the Hensley and Co. beer distributorship in Phoenix. Her son Doug is a commercial airline pilot. And their daughter, Sidney, works in the music industry in Canada.

McCain was already contemplating a new career, a political life, when he left the Navy. He had concluded that he may not be following in all of the footsteps of his "first heroes," his father and grandfather, the admirals. In the years after the initial physical therapy that had enabled him to fly again, his condition "had deteriorated to the point that neither I nor anyone else ever thought I would fly again," he wrote in "Worth the Fighting For." "Some of my Navy friends believed I could still earn my star; others doubted it. But even had I made Rear Admiral, the fact that I was permanently grounded would preclude my command of a carrier or battle group, making further promotion impossible."

McCain retired from the Navy in 1981, after 22 years. His father had died in March of that year. His move to Arizona opened up a new political opportunity. By virtue of its growth, the state was gaining a new congressional district, and McCain eyed it early on. But the new district was drawn in Tucson. So when the 1982 elections offered an open seat near Phoenix, in Mesa, with the retirement of former House Minority Leader John Rhodes (R-Ariz.), Cindy McCain bought the couple a house inside the district, and McCain lent his campaign $169,000 from her trust fund. It wasn't an easy race. Two seasoned state legislators wanted the seat. So did a civic activist in Mesa. But McCain finished first in the Republican primary, with 15,363 votes, about 3,000 more than his closest rival. And in the solidly Republican district, he beat his Democratic opponent by more than 2-1.

A second career was born, when he was 46.

McCain arrived in the House chambers of the Capitol in January 1983 as no stranger. He had finished his Navy career as the senior naval liaison to the Senate — a post his father had held many years before. He still carried the aura of a celebrated POW. He was elected president of the House GOP's freshman class. He had no trouble with re-election to a second term.

Early in his second term, McCain returned to Vietnam with another camera crew — this one headed by CBS News' Walter Cronkite. In Hanoi, McCain and Cronkite paused at a monument marking the capture of "the famous air pirate" shot down in 1967. It was a monument to McCain, but this time the crowd surrounding him by the lake in Hanoi was looking for celebrity handshakes.

DEFYING THE PRESIDENT

Although McCain arrived in Washington in the mold of a Reagan Republican, he also bucked his party's president early on. His first year in the House, he voted against a resolution permitting Reagan to keep Marines in Lebanon for 18 more months. He spoke out against the president's plans in a speech on the House floor: "What can we expect if we withdraw from Lebanon? The same as will happen if we stay. ... I also recognize that our prestige may suffer in the short term, but I am more concerned with our long-term national interests. ... I am not calling for an immediate withdrawal of our forces. What I desire is as rapid a withdrawal as possible. I do not foresee obtainable objectives in Lebanon. I believe the longer we stay, the more difficult it will be to leave. I am prepared to accept the consequences of our withdrawal."

The resolution passed 270-161, just a month before the bombing of the Marine barracks in Beirut that killed 241.

In his 2002 memoir, McCain suggested that his vote was no "act of political courage" — the resolution's passage was assured. But McCain also suggested that it made the media interested now in something more than a mere former POW. He was drawing invitations to debate the matter on PBS and in the columns of The New York Times and The Washington Post: "It came at little cost to my political ambitions. It actually benefited my career a little ..."

"As events turned out, my opposition to the president would prove to be well-founded," McCain wrote in "Worth the Fighting For." "But by then I could take little solace in the soundness of my judgment. Whatever confidence it gave me was offset by a nagging sense of something close to shame that my opposition had had little greater effect than to profit me personally by raising my national profile."

A freshman Republican, especially one who had served as a military officer, was expected to support the commander in chief, McCain has noted. In addition, his "disdain of congressional interference in the conduct of the war in Vietnam" had only increased his own "natural antipathy to the notion of 535 self-styled secretaries of defense second-guessing and hamstringing the president's authority in national security matters. I would have much preferred giving the president my support, had I thought his policy had a chance in hell of being successful."

McCain also wrote these words in 2002 that would come to have greater significance for his ultimate campaign ahead:

"The description *quagmire* is an overused cliché since it became a synonym for the Vietnam War. It is routinely, and often ridiculously, applied to most conflicts where the application of American military force is considered. And no sooner is one conflict *unquagmired* by force of American arms than the term is again hastily invoked to warn against entry into another."

4 *The Senator: "I cast a lot of hard votes"*

SEN. BARRY GOLDWATER, the five-term senator from Arizona, archetypal modern-day conservative and Republican nominee for president in 1964, wouldn't seek re-election in 1986. And Rep. John McCain, the two-term House member who had lived in Arizona just six years, now his longest place of residence, wanted the seat.

McCain got lucky when Gov. Bruce Babbitt, a popular Democrat, decided against seeking Goldwater's seat. And McCain got a clear pass at his own party's nomination. He faced, in the general election, Democrat Richard Kimball, a telegenic former state senator from Phoenix. McCain's "irremediable" sense of humor, as The Arizona Republic recounted the race, offered his rival at least one good opening: Addressing an audience in Tucson, McCain referred to Leisure World, a retirement golf community in

Sen. John McCain confers outside a Senate Republican policy luncheon at the U.S. Capitol in May 2005. McCain voted with Republicans on many social issues — most notably abortion — but parted ways with them on some others.

Mesa, as "Seizure World." In the last election, McCain joked, 97 percent of the residents had voted and "the other 3 percent were in intensive care." Rival Kimball, asserting that he was "offended by his joke," also seized on McCain's zero rating from the National Council for Senior Citizens. McCain learned something about rapid-response in that episode, writing later that the "Seizure World" gaffe "would have passed a hell of a lot faster if I had listened to my advisers and apologized immediately." He also attributed the comment to his own irrepressible trait: "Wiseass."

McCain's opponent also attacked his newfound family's business, one of the biggest Anheuser-Busch distributors in the nation, and the source of some of McCain's early political money. McCain was outraising and outspending Kimball at least 4-1. Kimball trotted out old newspaper accounts showing that Cindy Hensley's father, Jim, had once worked for a rich rancher and political power broker named Kemper Marley Sr. Jim Hensley, a bombardier in a B-17 shot down over the English Channel during World War II, had returned to work with his brother at Marley-owned liquor distributorships in Phoenix and Tucson. In 1948, the Hensley brothers were convicted of falsifying records to conceal illegal distribution of hundreds of cases of liquor between 1945 and 1947, according to government lawyers. The brother drew a year's sentence in prison, Jim Hensley six months. His sentence was suspended, and he served probation. In 1953, Jim Hensley again was charged with falsifying records at Marley's firms. The firms hired a defense lawyer: William Rehnquist, later to become chief justice of the Supreme Court. Hensley was acquitted.

McCain beat his opponent by 20 percentage points. At age 50, he took his first seat in the Senate, as well as seats on the Armed Services, Commerce and Indian Affairs Committees.

THE "KEATING FIVE" SCANDAL

But it took just months for Sen. McCain to confront the political scandal of his nascent career. Charles Keating, a high-flying home builder in Arizona who had befriended and entertained McCain and other politicians, wanted to head off federal regulators who were moving in early 1987 to take over the failing Lincoln Savings and Loan, a subsidiary of his American Continental Corp. Keating had contributed thousands of dollars to the campaigns of Arizona's senior senator, Democrat Dennis DeConcini. In March of that year, Keating asked DeConcini to convene a meeting with the thrift regulators and urge them to leave Lincoln alone. DeConcini arranged a meeting with not only the regulators, but also four other senators, including McCain.

McCain (right) listens as Sen. Russell Feingold (D-Wis.) acknowledges him during an event to celebrate the eventual passage of the McCain-Feingold campaign finance reform bill in March 2002 on Capitol Hill.

In Chicago, McCain campaigns for David McSweeney, Republican candidate for Illinois' 8th Congressional District, in October 2006.

McCain had met Keating, a fellow Navy flier, a few years back. Keating had sponsored a fundraiser for McCain's first congressional campaign in 1982, raising more than $11,000 from employees of American Continental. In 1983, as McCain prepared for re-election without any prospect of a serious challenge, Keating sponsored at $1,000-per-plate dinner for his campaign. And in 1986, Keating raised $50,000 for McCain's Senate race. By 1987, according to The Arizona Republic's count, McCain had collected about $112,000 in contributions from Keating and associates. The newspaper also found that a partnership involving McCain's wife and father-in-law had invested $359,000 in a shopping center that Keating developed in 1986, and that the McCains had made at least nine trips aboard the American Continental jet, including three for vacations at Keating's retreat in the Bahamas. McCain did not pay Keating for some of the trips — at a cost of about $13,000 — until years afterward, after learning that Keating was in trouble.

Keating had a list of demands for federal regulators, but McCain told Keating that all he intended to do was attend the meeting to see if Keating was being treated fairly. The first session, on April 2, 1987, in DeConcini's office, included McCain and Democratic Sens. John Glenn of Ohio and Alan Cranston of California. The four senators met with the chairman of the Federal Home Loan Bank Board, Ed Gray. He told the senators that, as chairman of the board, he had no personal knowledge of Lincoln's situation but would defer to regulators based in San Francisco.

In the next meeting, on April 9, a fifth senator joined in, Democrat Donald Riegle of Michigan. Among them, the five had collected $300,000 in campaign contributions from Keating. The five met with James Cirona, president of the Federal Home Loan Bank of San Francisco, and two other federal regulators. William Black, deputy director of the Federal Savings and Loan Insurance Corp., attended the meeting — which he later called a show of force by Keating — and told the Republic that Keating hoped senators could pressure the regulators to drop their case against Lincoln. "The Senate is a really small club, like the cliché goes," Black told the newspaper. "And you really did have one-twentieth of the Senate in one room, called by one guy, who was the biggest crook in the S&L debacle."

Black also kept notes of the meeting and quoted McCain as saying in that second session: "One of our jobs as elected officials is to help constituents in a proper fashion. [American Continental] is a big employer and important to the local economy. I wouldn't want any special favors for them ... I don't want any part of our conversation to be improper." Still, Black maintained that the regulators were nervous about the senators' intentions. "They were all different in their own way," he told the newspaper. "McCain was always Hamlet ... wringing his hands about what to do."

The other senators were more direct: Glenn telling the regulators to charge Lincoln or leave it alone, DeConcini calling it unusual for regulators to be putting a company out of business. But the regulators advised the senators that Lincoln's abuses were so serious that they were sending a criminal referral to the Justice Department. "This is an extraordinarily serious matter," one said.

McCain was finished with the matter after this meeting. He maintained later that he had been "troubled by the appearance of the meeting" and "only wanted them to be fairly treated."

The government's case against Lincoln moved forward, though it was taken out of the San Francisco-based regulators' hands and moved to Washington. In April 1989, the government seized the bankrupt Lincoln. Its federal bailout, $2 billion, was the costliest of the nationwide S&L scandal. In 1990, Keating was charged with 42 counts of fraud. In 1993, a federal jury convicted him of 73 counts of wire and bankruptcy fraud and sentenced him to more than 12 years in prison. He served about four years before the conviction was overturned, and in 1999, at age 75, he pleaded guilty to four counts of fraud and was credited for time served.

The senators had become known as the "Keating Five." The Senate Ethics Committee opened hearings on their conduct in November 1990. In February 1991, the panel found "substantial credible evidence" of misconduct by Cranston, saying he had "engaged in impermissible pattern of conduct in which fundraising and official activities were substantially linked." It concluded that Riegle and DeConcini had presented an appearance of impropriety but recommended no further action against them. The committee went even easier on Glenn and McCain, accusing them of "poor judgment" in the matter. After further hearings, in November the Ethics Committee voted to rebuke Cranston. He did not seek re-election in 1992, and he died in December 2000. The committee's counsel had wanted to drop McCain from the case, but leaders kept him in it to maintain an appearance of bipartisanship in the scandal. McCain later concluded: "I was judged eventually, after three years, of using, quote, poor judgment, and I agree with that assessment."

This became a transformative event for McCain, who launched his own bipartisan venture for reform of a tainted system of campaign financing as a result. After easily winning re-election to the Senate in 1992, he courted a reform-minded Democratic Sen. Russell Feingold of Wisconsin as a co-sponsor for campaign finance reform. If war had been the path to redemption for a young Navy flier who had built a personal reputation for rowdiness that he was intent on overcoming on an attack aircraft carrier, political reform could become the route to redemption for a senator who had stumbled in the weeds of campaign money and political influence during his freshman year in the Senate. And indeed, McCain's success at campaign finance reform — earning him new resentment within his own party, whose conservative leaders resisted any restraints on a system that enabled wealthy donors to pump unlimited amounts of cash into the coffers of the political parties — secured for him the image of a maverick reformer, supplanting the saga of the "Keating Five" in the media's eye. The resulting reform legislation, which became known as "McCain-Feingold," took years to enact. It started as a ban against "soft money," unlimited contributions to political parties, and a limitation on issue-oriented advertising run by unions and corporations within two months of Election Day. The ad restriction was panned as a threat to free speech and died in the first go-round of the legislation moving through the Senate. McCain and Feingold pressed the "soft money" ban. McCain argued that the unfettered system of campaign contributions was corrupt. Republican Sen. Mitch McConnell of Kentucky pressed McCain to name any corrupt senators. McCain indicted the whole system. The bill fell short of the votes needed for consideration on the Senate floor.

A REFORMER WORKING ACROSS PARTY LINES

When McCain was ready to wage his first campaign for president, in the fall of 1999, his efforts with Feingold had not only erased whatever blemish he had suffered in the "Keating Five" saga, but they had also imbued him with the image of a reformer.

He had worked across party lines on other matters — joining Democratic Sen. John Kerry of Massachusetts early in his first term in investigating charges that American prisoners of war or soldiers missing in action still remained in Vietnam. They found no such evidence. And with Kerry, also a decorated Navy veteran of the Vietnam War, McCain pressed for an end to the U.S. trade embargo with its erstwhile enemy and the re-establishment of diplomatic relations. President Bill Clinton announced a formal normalization of U.S. relations with Vietnam in July 1995. The government still lists more than 1,700 Americans as unaccounted for in Southeast Asia, including 1,350 in Vietnam.

Failing in his first bid for the Republican presidential nomination in 2000, McCain returned to the Senate.

On Capitol Hill, Sen. McCain greets Sen. Barack Obama (D-Ill.) before Obama's testimony to the Senate Committee on Environment and Public Works in January 2007.

And he returned immediately to campaign finance reform. In March 2001, two weeks of debate ensued, with McCain and Feingold fending off many hostile amendments. The Republican leadership opposed the bill. The White House opposed it. Unions opposed it. Many Democrats, who had grown as adept at raising "soft money" as the Republicans had, also opposed it. Elizabeth Drew, a writer who followed the debate, concluded that it never would have passed if Democrats had been able to cast secret ballots. In "Citizen McCain," Drew wrote of one Democrat who told her that the bill had "taken on a life that's larger than the legislation because of McCain's presidential campaign. ... He's created a constituency for reform. So when my colleagues go home they'll have to do a lot of explaining if they vote against him."

McCain-Feingold passed the Senate on April 2 by 59-41. In the process, the limitation on individual contributions to federal candidates was raised from $1,000 and $2,000, and also adjusted for inflation each year. But the bill included both the "soft money" ban and issue-ad limitation. After extended fights, the House approved its version of the bill in February 2002, by 240-189. It was signed into law on March 2002. The Supreme Court initially supported the "soft money" ban but subsequently eroded the restrictions on issues ads.

"Against great odds, he did achieve the McCain-Feingold campaign finance reform bill and force a reluctant Bush to sign it," Drew wrote in "Citizen McCain." "But most Republicans hated the bill, feeling that it removed their advantage in raising money, and never forgave McCain for it."

This wasn't the last of McCain's bipartisan causes in the Senate. Along with Sen. Edward Kennedy (D-Mass.) and others, McCain became an ardent advocate of immigration reform. The Republican and the Democrat became the chief sponsors of a bill to overhaul the nation's immigration laws. The way McCain and his formerly bitter rival in the Republican primaries of 2000 — the newly elected president from Texas, George W. Bush — had defined it, this meant "comprehensive" immigration reform. And that meant tougher enforcement of the nation's borders while confronting the fact that an estimated 12 million undocumented immigrants already were living, and most working, in the United States. They supported some means of enabling "illegal aliens" who had work, had learned English and were free of any criminal records to eventually seek citizenship. They would ultimately get it passed by the Senate in 2006, only to see it die in the House, which had approved a bill focused on tougher border protection, in the run-up to midterm congressional elections. The unfinished

Sen. Ted Kennedy (D-Mass.) (from left), Sen. Carl Levin (D-Mich.) and Sen. McCain before a hearing of the Senate Armed Services Committee on the readiness of the Army and Marine Corps in February 2007.

measure has only become more controversial over time, with opponents accusing its sponsors of "amnesty" for illegal aliens.

"I cast a lot of hard votes, as did the other Republicans and Democrats who joined our bipartisan effort," McCain said in July 2007 in rebuttal to his Democratic rival for president, Sen. Barack Obama of Illinois, accusing McCain of backing away from the reform as it has grown more controversial. McCain, speaking about the importance of border protection, maintained that he remains committed to immigration reform. "I don't want to fail again to achieve comprehensive immigration reform," McCain said. "We must prove we have the resources to secure our borders and use them, while respecting the dignity and rights of citizens and legal residents of the United States. When we have achieved our border security goal, we must enact and implement the other parts of practical, fair and necessary immigration policy."

McCain voted with Republicans on many social issues — most notably abortion — but he parted ways with the president and others on some issues. For example, McCain opposed a constitutional amendment banning gay marriage, an issue Bush supported but never truly pressed. McCain also aligned with Democrats on many votes in the Senate. He sided with them on HMO regulation in 2001, and he and Kennedy and former Democratic Sen. John Edwards of North Carolina sponsored an HMO "patients' bill of rights." McCain, an avowed opponent of the "earmarks" and "pork-barrel" spending that congressmen like to insert in virtually any bill they can find, cast the sole Republican vote against a water-projects bill in 2001, complaining that it held $1.2 billion worth of special projects that had been earmarked for districts. And he has been vocally critical of the 2008 farm bill, replete with subsidies such as a $93 million tax break for thoroughbred race horse owners that he has ridiculed on the campaign trail. McCain, campaigning, was not present for the final votes on the farm bill.

McCain's divide with Bush ran deep. Opposing the president on an issue Bush had staked out early in his first term, McCain supported federal funding for research involving embryonic stem cells. With Kerry, he proposed new federal fuel-mileage standards for cars and light trucks. And, in 2001, McCain was one of only two Republicans to vote against the president's first tax cuts,

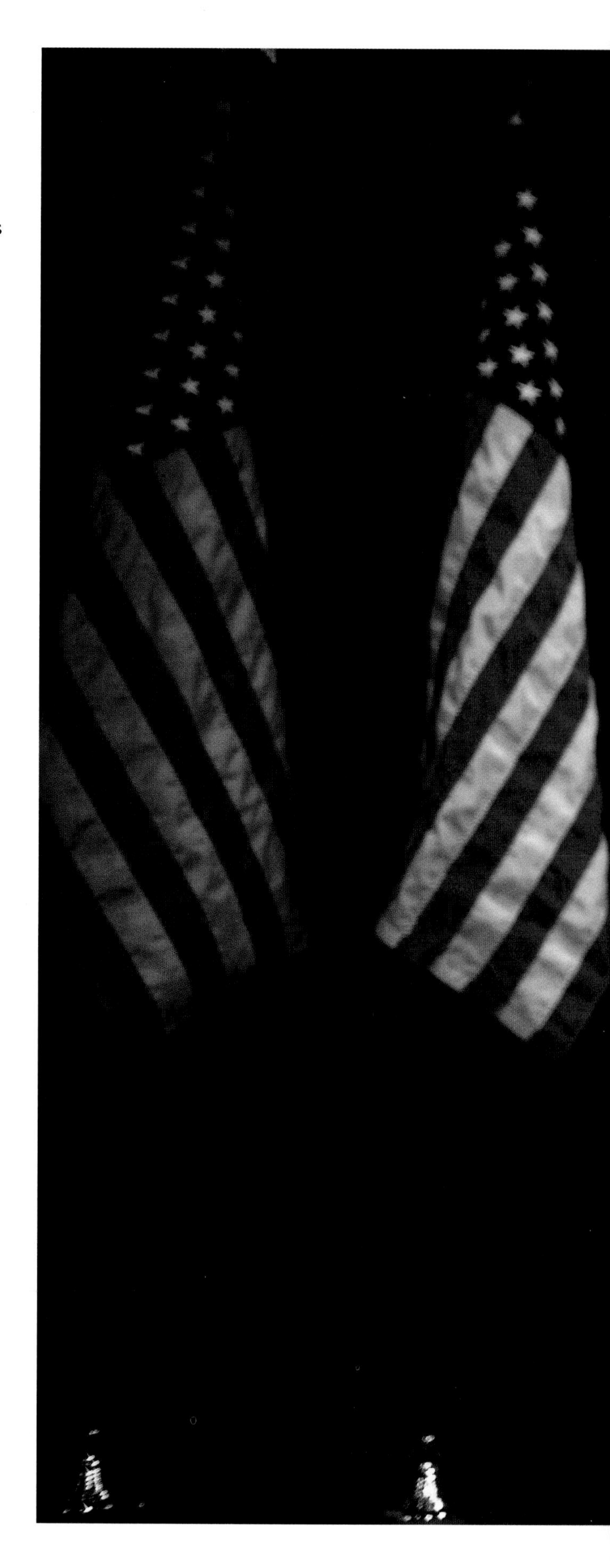

McCain speaks at the Center for Strategic and International Studies in April 2007 in Washington. He warned of U.S. reliance on foreign oil.

arguing that the breaks in the $1.35 trillion, 10-year bill were too heavily weighted toward the wealthiest Americans. All the House's Republicans had approved the president's tax cuts, the biggest since Ronald Reagan's in 1981, and 28 Democrats had joined them there. In the Senate, 12 Democrats sided with Bush on the tax cuts, and Sen. Lincoln Chafee of Rhode Island was the other Republican opposed. McCain said at the time: "I cannot in good conscience support a tax cut in which so many of the benefits go to the most fortunate among us at the expense of middle-class Americans who most need tax relief."

Later, McCain went on to support the president's next round of tax cuts and has advocated their extension — particularly the repeal of the estate tax. If Congress does not act, the estate tax abolished in Bush's tax cuts will be reinstated. "I believe that the estate tax is an onerous and confiscatory tax," McCain said at a campaign event this year. "Everything you've worked for all your life can literally be taken away by the federal government. ... 'Death tax' is a better description," said McCain, who likes to joke that he worries "about sudden and unexpected deaths before that tax is reinstated."

When Sen. James Jeffords of Vermont left the Republican Party to become an Independent in 2001, tipping the balance of party power in a nearly evenly split Senate, McCain invited Democratic Sen. Tom Daschle of South Dakota, who was becoming the new Senate majority leader, to the McCain family ranch in the red rocks near Sedona, Ariz., fueling speculation that the Arizonan, too, might be on the verge of switching parties. Outgoing Senate Majority Leader Trent Lott, a Mississippi Republican, said at the time that he couldn't believe McCain might consider such a thing, "but, having said that, he has cast some votes on some issues" that questioned his party loyalty. "They just hung out and relaxed," a McCain spokeswoman said at the time, and McCain discounted any talk of switching parties — as well as talk that he might be considering another bid for the White House then. "I have no intention of running for president," McCain said in a statement released by his office on June 2, 2001, "nor do I have any intention of or cause to leave the Republican Party."

Bush had made immigration reform an early goal of his first term. But that and more fell by the wayside on Sept. 11, 2001. After the terrorist attacks on the World Trade Center in New York and the Pentagon outside Washington, McCain became an immediate supporter of Bush's military response. He pushed for additional ground troops in Afghanistan when the U.S. launched an attack against the Taliban regime and the sponsors of the terrorist attacks who were hiding in Afghanistan. McCain signed a letter with eight other members of Congress identifying the next target: Iraq.

"As we work to clean up Afghanistan and destroy Al Qaeda, it is imperative that we plan to eliminate the threat from Iraq," the nine wrote to the president on Dec. 6, 2001. "We believe we must directly confront Saddam [Hussein], sooner rather than later." The signers included McCain, Mississippi's Lott, then-Democratic Sen. Joe Lieberman of Connecticut, North Carolina Sen. Jesse Helms and then-House International Relations Chairman Henry Hyde, an Illinois Republican.

McCain also called for an investigation of the U.S. intelligence failures that preceded the attacks of 9/11. He suggested former Sens. Gary Hart of Colorado, who had led a commission warning of the threats of terrorism, and Warren Rudman of New Hampshire. McCain worked closely with the 9/11 Commission that was ultimately formed, pressuring the White House to increase its funding and release sensitive information.

"He was our No. 1 supporter in the Congress, and he took on everyone for us," Thomas Kean, chairman of the 9/11 Commission and a former Republican governor of New Jersey who would later campaign for McCain in 2008, said in an interview. "I heard him take on his own chairman in the Senate, late in the game, when we were coming up with recommendations for how the intelligence committees should operate, the chairman said everything is fine, and McCain looked him in the eye and said, 'That's not true.' He took on the White House for us." When the commission fought to get more money for its investigation, both the White House and Congress were balking, Kean said. "McCain held up the transportation bill single-handedly — the bill everyone really wanted to take home. ... He held it up until he heard from me that we had gotten what we needed for the commission."

THE IRAQ VOTE

McCain was among the 77 members of the Senate who voted for the authorization of the use of military force against Iraq in October 2002. But afterward, he would grow increasingly critical of the Bush administration's conduct of the war, calling for additional troops before Bush did. By December 2004, McCain was declaring that he had "no confidence" in Defense Secretary Donald Rumsfeld. A chorus of criticism for Rumsfeld rang out after the secretary confronted a soldier at a town hall-style meeting — McCain's own signature forum — on a tour of troops in Kuwait. Spec. Thomas Wilson of the 278th Armored Cavalry Regiment in the Tennessee National Guard told Rumsfeld that his unit had to scrounge metal plates from dumps to protect unarmored

"Against great odds, he did achieve the McCain-Feingold campaign finance reform bill and force a reluctant Bush to sign it. But most Republicans hated the bill, feeling that it removed their advantage in raising money, and never forgave McCain for it."

Author Elizabeth Drew

vehicles before taking them into Iraq. He asked why more armored vehicles were not available. Rumsfeld said the Army was working on it, but, "You go to war with the Army you have. They're not the Army you might want or wish to have at a later time."

McCain stopped short of calling for Rumsfeld's resignation — the president "can have the team that he wants around him," he told The Associated Press in an interview on Dec. 13, 2004. But he had said before that he had lost confidence in Rumsfeld: "My answer is still no. No confidence. ... I have strenuously argued for larger troop numbers in Iraq, including the right kind of troops."

And McCain, who had suffered 5½ years in the war prisons of Hanoi, became a vocal critic of the administration's defense of unfettered techniques in the interrogation of suspected terrorists. Although the Bush administration maintained that it was not condoning torture, McCain won an amendment banning it. The image of the United States—and the fate of future American prisoners of war—was at stake in this debate, he warned.

"We will not have as high a moral ground the next time we are in a conflict and Americans become ... prisoners of war," McCain said on NBC's "Meet the Press" in June 2005. "It worries me and it keeps me awake at night. It really does."

As he battled the White House over a torture ban overwhelmingly approved on Capitol Hill, McCain said in November 2005, "No one wants this issue to go away more than I. This issue is incredibly harmful to the United States of America and our image throughout the world."

While the White House was maintaining that the administration was not condoning torture, the president resisted McCain's efforts to attach a ban on torture to war-spending bills, insisting that its hands, particularly the hands of the CIA, could be tied in a war on terror that required harsh tactics. Following the initial revelations of the American military's abuse of prisoners at Abu Ghraib in Iraq, and the release of memos showing that the Justice Department had internally given the administration the green light for the toughest interrogation tactics necessary, McCain fought for an explicit ban on torture. Toward the end of 2005, the senior senator from Arizona vowed: "If necessary — and I sincerely hope it is not — I and the co-sponsors of this amendment will seek to add it to every piece of important legislation voted on in the Senate until the will of a substantial bipartisan majority in both houses of Congress prevails. Let no one doubt our determination."

After weeks of veto threats from the White House, Bush eventually reached an agreement with McCain: to include a ban on cruel, inhumane and degrading treatment in the U.S. Army's Field Manual for interrogation. In negotiations with the White House, McCain had agreed to legal protection for interrogators who had been carrying out orders. On Dec. 15, 2005, Bush made a highly public show of their sudden accord, inviting McCain and Senate Armed Services Committee Chairman John Warner of Virginia to the Oval Office. "Sen. McCain has been a leader to make sure that the United States of America upholds the values of America as we fight and win this war on terror," the president said during their visit to the White House. "And we've been happy to work with him to achieve a common objective, and that is to make it clear to the world that this government does not torture."

Yet Bush capped the torture-banning bill with one of his trademark "signing statements" that enable the administration to comply with laws as desired. And McCain later supported a larger bill containing an exemption carving the CIA out of the ban. The signing statement Bush added in late 2005 said: "The executive branch shall construe [the law] in a manner consistent with the constitutional authority of the President ... as Commander in Chief." This "will assist in achieving the shared objective of the Congress and the President ... of protecting the American people from further terrorist attacks."

The administration intended to reserve the right to employ harsher methods in special situations involving national security, a senior administration official told The Boston Globe, which had investigated the extent of Bush's signing statements: "We are not going to ignore this law," the official told the Globe. "We consider it a valid statute. We consider ourselves bound by the prohibition on cruel, unusual, and degrading treatment."

McCain also had been vocal about the need to hear

the cases of hundreds of suspects captured at war and held at Guantanamo Bay, Cuba. "I know that some of these guys are terrible, terrible killers and the worst kind of scum of humanity," McCain had said of the Guantanamo detainees on "Meet the Press." "And there's a fear that if you release them that they'll go back and fight again against us. And that may have already happened. But balance that against what it's doing to our reputation throughout the world and whether it's enhancing recruiting for people to join Al Qaeda and other organizations that want to do bad things to the United States of America. I think, on balance, the argument has got to be ... that we've got to adjudicate these people's cases, and that means that if it means releasing some of them, you'll have to release them. Look, even Adolf Eichmann got a trial."

Yet McCain, who has supported the military tribunals that the Bush administration proposed for hearing the detainees' cases, spoke out forcefully in 2008 when the U.S. Supreme Court ruled 5-4 that detainees have a right to have their cases heard in federal court. McCain had helped craft the Military Commissions Act of 2006, which established a military system of trials as an alternative to civilian courts and prevented federal courts from hearing the habeas corpus petitions of detainees at Guantanamo. The court found part of that law in violation of the Constitution. McCain, campaigning for president in New Jersey in June, called it "one of the worst decisions in history. ... It opens up a whole new chapter and interpretation of our Constitution."

For all his criticism of the conduct of the war in its earlier phases — a "train wreck," McCain called it in January 2007 — McCain became an ardent supporter of the "surge" in U.S. forces that Bush announced that month in a nationally televised address.

"I am concerned about it, whether it is sufficient numbers or not," McCain said of the additional 21,500 troops that Bush first authorized. In an interview on "Meet the Press" on Jan. 21, 2007, McCain said: "I would have liked to have seen more. I looked Gen. [David] Petraeus in the eye and said, 'Is that sufficient for you to do the job?' He assured me that he thought it was and that he had been told that if he needed more he would receive them. I have great confidence in Gen. Petraeus. I think he's one of the finest generals that our military's ever produced. ... But do I believe that, if it had been up to me, would there have been more? Yes."

Referring to his comment in The Washington Post on Jan. 13 — that, "One of the most frustrating things that's ever happened in my political life is watching this train wreck" — he said on "Meet the Press": "Well, it's been a train wreck because, from the beginning, when the looting was allowed and then the [Iraqi] army was dissolved, and the so-called de-Baathification [the removal of Saddam Hussein's allies from the Iraqi government], there was a series of events which led to a steadily deteriorating situation. ... It's well-chronicled, the descent that we've been on, and so many people knew that this was a failed strategy. And that's why I think that this is our chance now, our last chance, to have a new strategy which will give us a chance to prevail."

Asked about opinion polls showing declining support for the war among the American public, McCain said in that January 2007 interview: "Americans are frustrated, they are angry and they are fed up. And what we need to do is show them a path to success. ... And also I think we need to make them more aware of the consequences of failure, which would be chaos in the region. And sooner or later, I think Americans might have to return. So I understand their frustration. I believe that President Bush now has the right strategy. I've been deeply disappointed in the strategy in the past, as is well-known, and I think this is our last chance."

"He was our No. 1 supporter in the Congress, and he took on everyone for us. I heard him take on his own chairman in the Senate."

Thomas Kean, chairman of the 9/11 Commission

5 *The Senator's Wife: "I am not as tough as he is"*

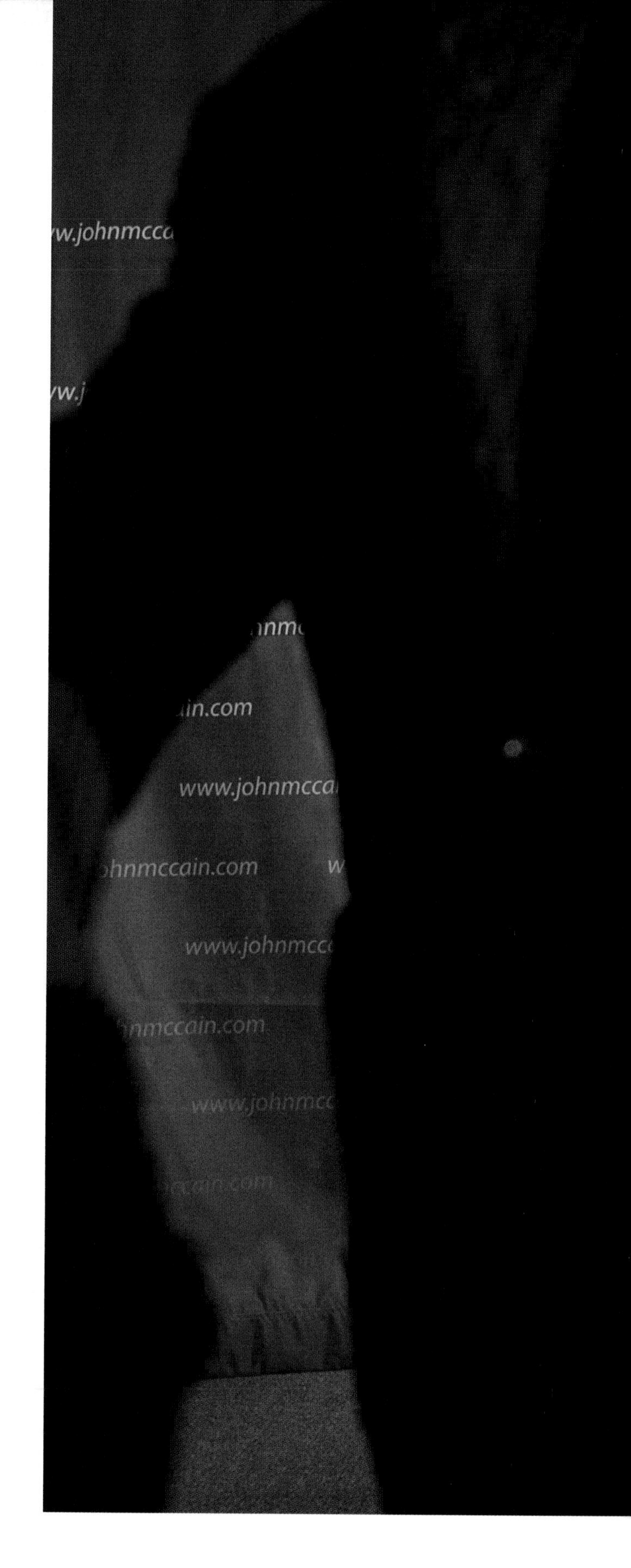

SEN. JOHN MCCAIN, "rootless" for much of his life, finally found a home in Arizona. "My ambition brought me to Arizona. ... I came to Arizona impatient to start a political career," McCain has written in his 2002 memoir, "Worth the Fighting For." He had considered a political course toward the end of his Navy career. And now he had both the base and the wherewithal to make that move.

But really it was Cindy Hensley who brought him there.

The globe-trotting and charity-minded heiress to a fortune now estimated at more than $100 million was a 24-year-old beer distributor's daughter when she met a swaggering naval captain at a cocktail party in Honolulu. McCain was her senior by 18 years. As the only child of Jim Hensley, one of the state's leading men, a bombardier during

Cindy McCain, at a March 2007 news conference in Mason City, Iowa, with her husband (foreground), was as reluctant about his first campaign for president as she was about his second.

Cindy McCain leaves a polling place with newborn daughter Meghan after voting in Tempe, Ariz., in November 1984.

John McCain with and his wife, Cindy, and their children (from left): Meghan, Bridget, Jimmy and Jack.

"Having a strong father, I wanted an older man, though John is 70 going on 30."

Cindy McCain

World War II who borrowed $10,000 to start a liquor business after the war and built one of the biggest Anheuser-Busch distributorships in the nation, she played a son's role in many ways: hiking in the backcountry of Arizona and camping along the Mexican border with her father. She was also crowned Junior Rodeo Queen of Arizona at 14. She left home for the University of Southern California, where she was a cheerleader and sorority sister and drove a gold Mercedes. She got a master's degree in special education and was groomed for the family business — she can tell if a beer is fresh by its taste. In spring 1979, on vacation in Hawaii, she accompanied her father, a onetime Army Air Corps bombardier, to a Navy reception, where McCain, the Navy's senior liaison to the Senate, had stopped during a trip to Asia. "I monopolized her attention the entire time," McCain wrote of the young woman he had met. Her parents were exceptionally gracious about it, he suggested: "I doubt I could match their graciousness should I find one of my daughters attracted to someone who reminded me of me."

The extent of the age difference wasn't completely clear to them until they applied for a marriage license a year later, she told Harper's Bazaar in 2007. "We discovered we'd both lied. I'd made myself three years older, he four younger," but she was perfectly comfortable with the time between them: "Having a strong father, I wanted an older man, though John is 70 going on 30. Last summer, he and our son Jack hiked the Grand Canyon rim to rim."

With McCain's marriage to the mother of his own three children falling apart — and he maintains that they were already separated when he started dating Cindy — he and Hensley had a long-distance relationship with trips between Washington and Phoenix. By April 1980, McCain and Carol Shepp would be divorced. By May 1980, McCain and Cindy Hensley would be married. McCain retired from the Navy in 1981 and took up a post with her father's firm, Hensley & Co., managing public relations and most of the company's advertising. By 1982, with his wife signing the contract on a house in the 1st Congressional District of Arizona, he would be waging his first campaign for Congress — with the help of his new wife's trust fund.

McCain had come from a family of seafaring officers and naval wives who were left at home to raise the children, and Cindy was soon to become a senator's wife who would raise his children and spend much of his Washington career at home in Arizona. "She had married a Navy captain, not a politician," McCain has written. "Neither she nor I really appreciated how demanding my new career would be and how seriously it would affect our home life. We didn't have children when I decided to run for office, but we were planning to start a family. Like the Navy, politics would separate me by time and distance from those I love most, and my wife would bear the disproportionate share of the responsibility for raising our children. She has raised our four children beautifully."

The first-born, Meghan, arrived in October 1984. She would graduate from Columbia University and blog on her father's presidential campaign. John Sidney McCain IV was born in 1986 and is near completion of his course at the U.S. Naval Academy — the fourth in a line of academy men with the same name. Jimmy was born in 1988, enlisted in the Marines at 17 and has been deployed to and returned home from Iraq. Bridget, brought to the U.S. as a newborn in 1991 from an orphanage in Bangladesh on a journey that Cindy McCain made there, was adopted by the McCains in 1993.

They have a home in Phoenix and a 13-acre ranch compound in a scenic setting near Sedona.

AVERSE TO POLITICS

Cindy McCain, who has suffered personal hardships during some of her husband's roughest times in Washington and on the campaign trail, and who had a stroke in 2004, admits to having less of an appetite for politics than her husband. "I'm not as tough as he is," she told the Chicago Tribune's Jill Zuckman. The senator's wife recalled his first approach to her, in mid-2006, about making his second bid for the White House. She partly hoped that he would think twice about it. But six months later, after opening their Christmas presents, the McCains held a family meeting in the living room to talk about it. The children were there. So was the senator's mother, Roberta McCain. Bridget, whose image had been invoked in the 2000 presidential campaign when an underground smear campaign accused McCain of having an illegitimate black daughter, wanted to know how he might confront new personal attacks. Cindy McCain recalled opponents portraying her husband as mentally unstable as a result of his imprisonment during war.

In Manchester, Cindy and John McCain celebrate his victory in the New Hampshire primary in February 2000.

"It still affects me," she told Zuckman. "John says, 'Oh, don't let it bother you.' He's so good at that. He says, 'Oh, it's nothing, that's just the game.' Well, I'm not as tough as he is, and things like that do bother me. It's my husband, so it hurts. Unfortunately, it's part of politics, which I still don't like."

Initially, after her husband's first election to the House, Cindy McCain quit her job as a special education teacher and followed him to Washington. But she felt miscast there, as Newsweek has reported — younger, at 28, than some of her husband's own congressional staff, she suspected some were talking behind her back — a "trophy wife ... married for money." She was homesick and wanted to start a family but had suffered repeated miscarriages. The first time, she reached her husband on the House floor, and he took her to the hospital. The second and third time, they were apart. When she became pregnant again, in 1984, doctors' orders to stay off her feet and avoid travel dictated a simple move: Arizona. Since then, she has largely seen her husband on weekends, and mostly in Arizona.

On a scuba-diving vacation in Micronesia in 1984, Cindy McCain had first been moved to do more than work with disabled students back home. A friend suffered an injury, and they went to an island hospital. It was rat-infested and lacked both an X-ray machine and beds. When she got home, she arranged for medical supplies to be shipped there. Later, she assembled a medical team and returned to the hospital, the start of a long interest in medical relief missions abroad. She has traveled to Kuwait, Nicaragua, Rwanda, Bangladesh and Vietnam, before the U.S. normalized relations, and most recently, in 2008, she traveled to Kosovo.

At the same time, she had attempted to conceal from her husband her own health problems. Back surgery and lingering pain and another undiagnosed malady led to an addiction to painkillers, Percocet and Vicodin. She had gotten the drugs from the supplies of her own charity,

Cindy McCain travels with her husband on a South Carolina campaign swing in September 2007.

the American Voluntary Medical Team, which she had founded in 1988. Because her husband was coming home only on weekends, she avoided complaining about her pain — particularly as he was facing scrutiny during the "Keating Five" investigation. "Because I only saw him on the weekends and I didn't want him to come home to this woman who couldn't do anything, I completely masked it and completely kept myself somewhat pain-free and [with] the ability to function and do everything he wanted," she said in her Tribune interview.

In August 1994, the senator's political strategist summoned some Arizona reporters to the senator's home. Cindy McCain, then 40, told them that she had been a drug addict from 1989 to 1992. She blamed not only her back surgeries, but also the pain of the "Keating Five" scandal. The Arizona Republic, often critical of the senator, had not been invited. Yet, as the Republic has recounted the meeting, the Drug Enforcement Administration had found irregularities in an audit of the charity's medical records. She emotionally described how federal agents had shown up at her door, asking about the missing pills. In an agreement with the U.S. attorney's office, she was not charged with a crime but agreed to perform community service. She also told the reporters that she had entered The Meadows, a drug-treatment center, and had gone to anti-dependency meetings twice a week. In 1993, she said, she underwent a hysterectomy that ended the back pain.

"I was stunned," John McCain said at the time. "Naturally, I felt enormous sadness for Cindy and a certain sense of guilt that I hadn't detected it. I feel very sorry for what she went through, but I'm very proud she was able to come out of it."

Cindy McCain, asked why she had gone public with the problem, told the reporters assembled in her house: "If what I say can help just one person to face the problem, it's worthwhile. They should know it's OK to be scared. It's OK to talk about it."

She had taken her charity to the Kuwaiti desert in the days after the end of the Persian Gulf War, in 1991, delivering medical supplies to refugees. The same year, she had visited Mother Teresa's orphanage in Dhaka, Bangladesh. In a home for 160 abandoned newborns, the nuns handed her one infant with a heart defect, another with a cleft palate. She sought visas to take both girls home, by her account in an interview with Harper's Bazaar, and was refused permission when one official told her that they could perform surgery on one of the children. "Then do it! What are you waiting for?" she demanded, slamming a fist on a table. The stunned official signed the papers. "I don't know where I got the nerve," she told Harper's. When she returned to Phoenix with

"Like the Navy, politics would separate me by time and distance from those I love most, and my wife would bear the disproportionate share of the responsibility for raising our children."

John McCain

the child suffering from a cleft palate, the senator met her at the airport. Before she had returned, she realized, "I couldn't give up this child." She had telephoned her husband to tell him about the two children. "When I disembarked carrying Bridget, John said, under his breath, 'Where's she going?' I said, 'To our house.' He laughed. 'I thought so.'" They adopted the girl, a thriving teenager now. And family friends adopted the other child.

The senator's wife was as reluctant about his first campaign for president as she was about his second. But she also discovered a certain enjoyment in the travels of his first campaign's trademark "Straight Talk Express," a roving campaign bus that carried a full complement of inquiring reporters. "For most of the 20 years we've been married, he's been in Washington all week while I'm in Arizona with the kids," she told The New York Times in early 2000. "I've never spent this much time with my husband."

And this time around, she told Harper's Bazaar in 2007, McCain had sold her with some sweet talk: "John said something so lovely — from his perspective. I don't believe it myself. He said: 'I think you could bring style, grace and elegance back to the White House.' Those words had never come out of his mouth before. And I thought, 'That's how he sees me.' Knowing he believes in me that way gives me a great deal of strength."

Still, she has said that she refrains from active involvement in the business of the campaign. At an annual Conference for Women in October 2007 sponsored by Maria Shriver, wife of California Gov. Arnold Schwarzenegger, Cindy McCain joined the wives of several other presidential candidates of both parties. Noting how busy her husband is, between Congress and the campaign, she said that when he came home on Friday nights, "The last thing I was going to do was to talk about issues with him."

Yet the voters, Cindy McCain suggested, are not only selecting a new president, but also weighing a potential first lady. Bill Clinton had said in 1992 that voters would be getting "two for the price of one" with him and his wife, Hillary. And voters may well have considered that calculus during the Democratic Party primaries of 2008, when Sen. Hillary Clinton of New York was seeking the presidential nomination and her husband was campaigning for her. "I think the American people truly ... take this in the right way — electing both people," Cindy McCain said at the women's forum staged by California's first lady. "But from the spouse standpoint, not in a position of leadership or decision-making ... they do, I believe, look at you both very carefully — and your families."

She has her work cut out for her. She is chairwoman of Hensley & Co., the third-largest Anheuser-Busch distributor. And she has her charities, in addition to those in which she is personally involved. IRS reports show that she and her husband have together donated to charities — giving more than $200,000 in 2007 — including their children's schools, research on AIDS, heart disease, Parkinson's disease and Down syndrome. She sits on the boards of HALO Trust, a Scotland-based organization dedicated to the removal of land mines, and Operation Smile, which lines up plastic surgeons for children with cleft palates and other birth defects, and has been on the board of CARE, which fights world poverty. "I'm not the Ford Foundation," she told the Tribune, "but I do what I can."

In New Hampshire, John and Cindy McCain sit on the "Straight Talk Express" campaign bus with reporters on primary day in January 2008.

McCAIN
McCAIN
McCAIN
JOHNMcCAIN.COM
McCAIN
JOHNMcCAIN.COM

In March 2008, workers from the HALO Trust show Cindy McCain minefields in Kosovo that haven't been cleared. She is on the board of HALO Trust, which is dedicated to the removal of land mines.

6 *Seeking the White House: "We are creating a new majority"*

JOHN MCCAIN, the war hero and political lone ranger, had made a name for himself in Washington that readily translated into rich material for an upstart presidential campaign. He was fiercely independent and tough. He spoke his mind. He had a disarming sense of humor. He worked with Republicans and Democrats alike, whatever it took to get something done. But it also appeared that McCain might most enjoy working for himself. If the highest ranks of naval command had eluded him during his first career, partly because of a long imprisonment and lasting injuries, partly because of an irrepressible individualistic streak, he was not going to be content to settle for middle ranks in the realm of political command. He was aiming for commander in chief.

Twice McCain counted on the famously

Campaigning for the nomination, McCain (right) appears at a bridge dedication on Veterans Day 1999 in Merrimack, N.H.

V.F.W.

"Neither party should be defined by pandering to the outer reaches of American politics and the agents of intolerance, whether they be Louis Farrakhan or Al Sharpton on the left, or Pat Robertson or Jerry Falwell on the right."

John McCain

stubborn, independent-minded voters of New Hampshire to propel his bids for the White House. And twice the voters of the Granite State came through for McCain, the senior senator from Arizona.

The first time around, in 2000, the Republican railing against special interests in Washington had little choice but to bypass the contest-starting presidential nominating caucuses of Iowa. McCain has long opposed the subsidies and tax breaks of "pork-barrel" spending and made it clear that he was no fan of federal ethanol subsidies. In corn-growing Iowa, this was a self-imposed political death sentence. Still, McCain's "Straight Talk Express" would weave a wandering course through an ethanol minefield. When his second campaign arrived, McCain was ready to talk about the importance of ethanol: "I see a bright future for ethanol," he declared in 2007. Yet again in 2008, after the primaries had concluded and he had clinched his party's nomination, he would cite ethanol subsidies in a massive new federal farm bill as among the evils of a measure that most senators supported — "I certainly don't think we should be subsidizing ethanol," he said at a campaign rally in mid-July. However, the campaigning McCain was not present for the final farm bill votes in 2008 as it was approved overwhelmingly.

New Hampshire offered something custom-tailored for the self-styled maverick: presidential primary elections open to any and all voters. McCain was attempting in 2000, as he would again in 2008, to assemble a coalition of centrist Republicans, Democrats and independents — he called it, at first, "a McCain majority."

For McCain, appealing to the freewheeling voters of New Hampshire who could take either party's ballot, the state held gold. In his first bid for the Republican presidential nomination, he formally announced his candidacy in Nashua, N.H., on Sept. 27, 1999. He stumped in the state 71 times, amassing a growing base of support at 114 fervent town hall rallies before delivering a punishing blow to his party's putative front-runner, the heavily financed, Iowa caucus-winning governor from Texas and son of a former president, George W. Bush. McCain beat Bush by 19 percentage points in the first primary election of 2000. The state would become the linchpin of his presidential campaigns. McCain would also formally launch his next campaign in New Hampshire. And in the summer of 2007, when McCain's second campaign was near bankruptcy, jettisoning consultants and staffers to stay afloat, he climbed aboard a coach flight to New Hampshire to dig in anew. By the time New Hampshire cast the first party primary votes of 2008, McCain was running several points ahead of another well-financed rival from neighboring Massachusetts, former Gov. Mitt Romney, in a crowded GOP field.

McCain's appeal to independents was a matter of political necessity. Over many years in the Senate, he had alienated conservatives with the causes he had taken on, often displaying a capacity to buck his own party's presidents. In his first party contest, which became a two-way race with Bush, he faced a rival actively courting the conservative base of the GOP, a campaign that reached a fever pitch in the Christian conservative precincts of South Carolina's second primary. Bush, in a rebound from his New Hampshire loss to McCain, had made one of his first stops in the Palmetto State at Bob Jones University, a Christian campus that long banned interracial dating. McCain, for his part, seemed to go out of his way to alienate conservative Christians, who make up 4 in 10 of his party's voters. When the Religious Right lined up against him, he cast the televangelists, most notably Jerry Falwell and his Moral Majority, as "agents of intolerance." And McCain paid for all that in South Carolina in 2000, where the Bush campaign was bolstered by a vicious smear campaign that personally attacked McCain and his family. Only in Michigan, again open to all voters, could McCain regain some of the steam of his challenge to Bush, who effectively won the nomination in the Super Tuesday spree of primaries that year and clinched the next week.

"A CRUSADE"

McCain and Bush waged a personally bitter campaign. "It's not a campaign any more. It's a crusade," McCain had said as he carried his contest with Bush into South Carolina. Dismissing suggestions that his stunning win in New Hampshire was "a bump in the road," he said in South Carolina: "I'm telling you, my friends, it was a land mine." Bill Rauch, mayor of Beaufort, S.C., told McCain

McCain chats with diners after a Veterans Day breakfast in Laconia, N.H., in 1999.

supporters at a rally shrouded by old live oaks: "This man is fearless. In this party, we need a reformer in the spirit of Teddy Roosevelt, in the spirit of Ronald Reagan." Yet there remained some untouchable issues for McCain and Bush in this campaign, both deferring to South Carolina on the fate of the Confederate flag flying atop the Capitol in Columbia. It was a hot issue in that year's primaries, more so in the Democratic contest, dominated there by African-American voters. McCain called the Stars and Bars "offensive" and "a symbol of racism and slavery," but also "a symbol of heritage." Months later, after his ultimate loss to Bush, he would return to Columbia to acknowledge that he had dodged the question and "compromised" his own principles — the flag should come down, he said. And it did, that July.

McCain had successfully appealed to voters young and old. The Stars and Stripes was flying for McCain at one evening rally in the atrium of the engineering school in Columbia, where Mandy Reeves, a 20-year-old native of South Carolina who was bound for the Navy at the time, said: "I feel really and truly that he is giving people of all age groups someone to believe in." She added: "I wish I had my uniform on. I would have stood up to salute."

For all the tumult of that contest, Mike Murphy, McCain's media adviser at the time and a friend with no role in the campaign under way in 2008, remembered a tireless campaigner with an indefatigable sense of humor. "Candidate schedules wear these guys down," Murphy said, recalling a tale from the 2000 trail. "We were in South Carolina in some Motel 6. ... It was 1:30 in the morning. [McCain] was standing there in his boxer shorts and had to do a [phone] call. ... And then we tell

Following page
Cindy and John McCain change buses in January 2000 after theirs broke down in the snow outside Hillsborough, N.H.

Mc
PAID

CAIN
CAIN 2000, INC.

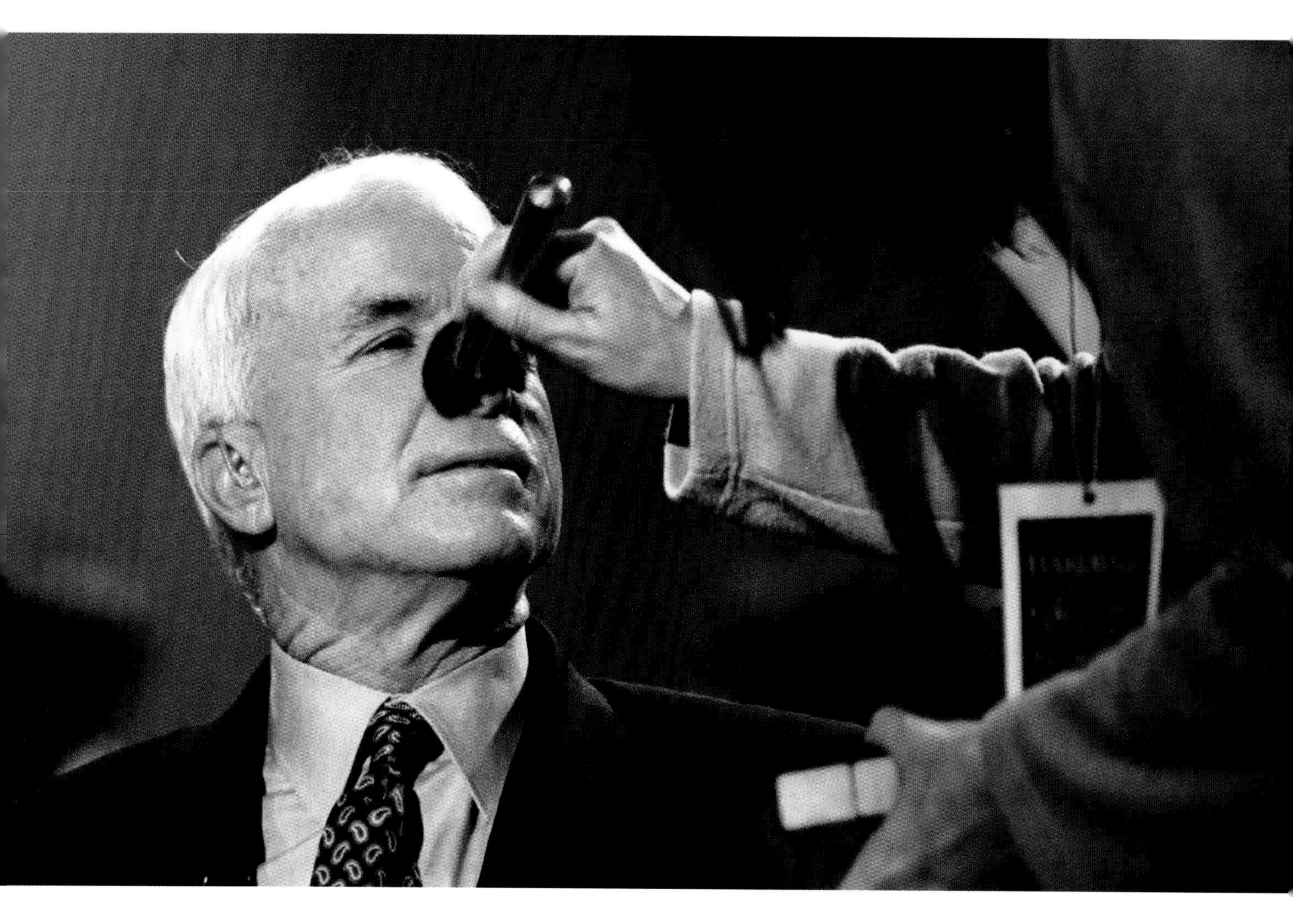

McCain is readied for a TV appearance at Clemson University in South Carolina in February 2000.

him, 'Bad news, your day starts two hours earlier in the morning than it was supposed to.' And McCain looked at us, and looked at his feet, and looked up and said, 'You're telling me I'm only going to get three hours of sleep? Well, boys, we can do that standing on our head.'"

Bush, regrouping his advisers in Texas after his loss to McCain in New Hampshire, re-emerged in South Carolina as the self-described "reformer with results." He even announced his own plans for campaign finance reform, which McCain and Sen. Russell Feingold of Wisconsin had pursued without success before the 2000 elections. This would include a ban on donations to members of Congress from lobbyists while Congress was in session and restrictions on union- and corporate-funded campaign advertising. This was a not-so-thinly-veiled jab at McCain, who was chairman of the Senate Commerce Committee and had accepted contributions from lobbyists while complaining about the "soft money" that they give to political parties. "This business about limiting individuals' capacity to run ads on the air ... it's their right to do so," Bush said. "This is America."

Bush portrayed McCain as the ultimate Washington power player, as opposed to the maverick McCain was playing on the campaign trail. Bush's TV ads called him "Chairman McCain" and maintained that he was cozy with lobbyists: "McCain solicits money from lobbyists with interests before his committee," said the narrator of a Bush campaign ad. It displayed a newspaper clipping: "McCain campaign is crawling with lobbyists."

McCain attempted to turn his opponent's negativity against him. "This is George Bush shaking hands with John McCain, promising not to run a negative campaign," the narrator of a McCain campaign ad in South Carolina stated. "Do we really want another politician in the White House America can't trust?"

But the ad wars weren't the least of it. When a 14-year-old boy answered a telephone call from a Bush backer calling McCain "a cheat, a liar and a fraud," the boy's mother contended at a McCain campaign rally in Spartanburg, S.C., her son was on the verge of tears.

McCain answers questions at a town hall meeting in North Charleston, S.C., in February 2000.

There were calls about McCain's adopted daughter, brought home from an orphanage in Bangladesh — attackers called her McCain's illegitimate black daughter. Some calls painted McCain's wife as a drug user. "Unfortunately, the race has turned ugly," allowed the script of a Bush campaign-sponsored phone call, while his campaign disavowed any connection to the worst of the tactics. "It has been brought to my attention that somebody has made phone calls on my behalf that call Sen. McCain a liar. ... I don't accept that kind of phone calling," Bush said at a fish fry in South Carolina. The Bush campaign enlisted a veterans' rights activist named Thomas Burch, accusing McCain of abandoning the veterans. He drew an organized rebuke from five senators who had served in Vietnam, including Sen. John Kerry, calling on Bush to "disassociate" himself from efforts to "impugn John McCain's character and so maliciously distort his record" — eerily auguring the challenge that Kerry, a decorated combat veteran, would face in his own campaign against President Bush in 2004, when the Swift Boat Veterans for Truth smeared Kerry's war record.

Bush beat McCain in South Carolina by about 11 percentage points, and by the time the race moved on to Michigan, again open to all voters, it was open season. McCain likened himself to Luke Skywalker going up against the Death Star, and vowed of his opponents at an arena in Saginaw: "We're gonna kill 'em." Bush told supporters at Detroit's Cobo Center: "You need to ask Sen. McCain why he is running the kind of campaign he is running." Bush maintained that McCain was riding "a high horse" down a "low road." McCain, with his reform-minded message, had been campaigning against the "iron triangle" of money, lobbying and lawmaking. But Bush insisted that McCain had "been ringing that iron triangle like a dinner bell." McCain called on voters to "reject this character assassination, reject the low road to the presidency."

McCain carried Michigan, and also his home state of Arizona, where he encouraged Republicans to join his coalition of centrist Democrats and independents. "This is where you belong," he told an audience at his victory party in his home state, "in the spirit of Teddy Roosevelt and Ronald Reagan. ... We are creating a new majority, my friends, a McCain majority."

VICTORY ELUSIVE

But as the contest moved toward Super Tuesday, with opportunities for open-primary voting diminishing, McCain was running out of venues for victory. He stepped up his own rhetoric, moving aggressively against the Religious Right's highest-profile leaders who had sided with Bush. In a campaign speech in Virginia Beach, Va., on Feb. 28, 2000, McCain declared that he had been maligned by the right's "agents of intolerance": "I am a pro-life, pro-family fiscal conservative, and advocate of a strong defense. And yet Pat Robertson, Jerry Falwell and a few Washington leaders of the pro-life movement call me an unacceptable presidential candidate. They distort my pro-life positions and smear the reputations of my supporters. Why? Because I don't pander to them, because I don't ascribe to their failed philosophy that money is our message. ... Neither party should be defined by pandering to the outer reaches of American politics and the agents of intolerance, whether they be Louis Farrakhan or Al Sharpton on the left, or Pat Robertson or Jerry Falwell on the right."

"Observers thought the move politically unwise," McCain wrote of that speech in "Worth the Fighting For." "But I was proud of it and remain so." Yet, as he launched his next bid for the White House, in 2007, he also would be apologizing for it in some ways, attempting to make amends with Falwell.

On March 7, 2000, Bush carried 9 of the 13 states holding primaries and caucuses, and McCain's campaign was finished. It would be months before the primary rift between McCain and Bush would heal. But McCain delivered a speech backing Bush at the Republican National Convention in Philadelphia.

"It is easy to forget in politics where principle ends and selfishness begins," McCain told his party's convention on Aug. 1, 2000. "It takes leaders of courage and character to remember the difference." Bush, he said, was such a man. Many years ago, he said from the dais in Philadelphia, the governor's father, George H.W. Bush, had served in the Pacific under the command of McCain's grandfather. "Now it is my turn to serve under

On a bluff in Arizona, with wife Cindy at his side, John McCain announces his withdrawal from the presidential race in March 2000.

the son of my grandfather's brave subordinate," he said of George W. Bush, who had served as a fighter pilot, stateside, for the Texas Air National Guard during the war in Vietnam. McCain's grandfather had been an aviator, his father a submariner, he reminded the convention hall. His grandfather's final words to his father: "It's an honor to die for your country and your principles." McCain told his party, "I have been an imperfect servant of my country for over 40 years, and my many mistakes rightly humble me. But I am their son ... and they taught me to love my country, and that has made all the difference, my friends, all the difference in the world."

John McCain campaigns in Sanford, Fla., with George W. Bush, his former rival for the GOP nomination, in October 2000.

7 *The Nominee: "Recovering our principles"*

JOHN MCCAIN, who was approaching 64 as his party nominated Texas Gov. George W. Bush in 2000 for what would become an eight-year stint in the White House, underwent surgery for skin cancer that summer. It was the second time he fought the disease. He had suffered a less serious bout in 1993. In 2000, diagnosed with melanoma, he had two lesions removed from his arm and temple, leaving a permanent scar along the left side of his face.

But he would return to the Senate to complete his work on campaign finance reform, capping contributions to the parties and increasing what individuals could contribute to candidates. And it would have an immediate impact on the next election, restricting the riches of the parties, yet making the 2004

John and Cindy McCain board the "Straight Talk Express" after a town hall meeting in Peterborough, N.H., in January 2008.

contest between Bush and rival John Kerry of Massachusetts the costliest ever as each pushed the limits of their own contributors. Bush had entered the White House without a majority of the popular vote. He had won a slim Electoral College edge over former Vice President Al Gore after a disputed 537-vote margin for Bush in Florida resulted in a 36-day court battle over spoiled ballots that ultimately the Supreme Court had to resolve. The court ruled for Bush.

McCain, for all his public support of his party's new president, would not accept all of his agenda — McCain opposed Bush's first round of tax cuts in 2001 as too heavily weighted toward the wealthy — but he would align himself with the new president on national security in the face of a stunning crisis. By the end of Bush's first year in office, following the terrorist attacks of Sept. 11, 2001, the president's public approval had soared to a record high — 90 percent in the Gallup Poll — as a result of his forceful response to the attacks. And McCain now was squarely in Bush's camp, joining other congressional leaders in proposing an assault on Iraq's Saddam Hussein and joining a solid majority of senators who voted for the authorization of war.

Yet, as war was waged in Iraq, McCain grew disenchanted with the administration's conduct of it. He crossed swords with the White House over the interrogation of combatants captured overseas. And he became an outspoken critic of not only Secretary of Defense Donald Rumsfeld, but also Atty. Gen. Roberto Gonzales. And, as more Americans grew critical of the war in Iraq, the president's popularity steadily declined. When McCain was ready to publicly announce his next campaign for the White House, on March 1, 2007, the president's approval ratings had slumped — 33 percent in a Gallup Poll taken that March 2-3.

From the start, McCain set out to rekindle the spirit his first campaign had been known for. He was already assembling his campaign team when he made an appearance on CBS' "Late Show with David Letterman" to declare: "I am announcing that I will be a candidate for president of the United States." He smiled through the personal applause of the late-night talk show host sitting to his left as well as the adulation of the audience. After bandleader Paul Shaffer offered up a musical fanfare,

Outside City Hall in Manchester, N.H., John McCain stands by while his wife, Cindy, speaks to a crowd in January 2008.

Following page
The next day, Meghan, Cindy and John McCain celebrate his victory in the New Hampshire primary in Nashua.

www.johnmccain.com

www.johnmccain.com

MSNBC
MSNBC
MSNBC

Republican presidential candidates take the stage during a debate in Boca Raton, Fla., in January 2008. From left: Mitt Romney, John McCain, Rudy Giuliani, Ron Paul and Mike Huckabee.

The crowd cheers for McCain at a campaign rally at the Odeum Sports & Expo Center in Villa Park, Ill., in February 2008.

McCain suggested another tune: "Da, da... da, da.... da, da, da... da, da... da, da, da," sang McCain, and Shaffer readily complied with "Hail to the Chief."

This senator was no stranger to late-night comedy. He had hosted NBC's "Saturday Night Live." "They tell me I'm the first sitting senator ever to host this show," McCain said in his "SNL" monologue on Oct. 19, 2002. "They asked President Bush to do it, but apparently he doesn't like to work on weekends."

But was this a real announcement, Letterman asked? A formal announcement would follow, McCain replied. "You know, you drag this out as long as you can. You don't just have one rendition. You've got to do it over and over."

The day he made that formal announcement — once again in New Hampshire — he also made a point of drawing some distance between himself and his party's president. He dished out criticism for the war in Iraq that day, April 25, 2007, in Portsmouth, N.H. And later that day, with an appearance on CNN's "Larry King Live," he called on the attorney general to resign. At his formal announcement in New Hampshire, he said the United States "must never repeat" the mistakes it had made in Iraq. And, as for the attorney general: "I am very disappointed in his performance." He was prodded by King to say whether this meant that Gonzales should resign. "I think loyalty to the president should enter into his calculations," McCain replied. "I think that, out of loyalty to the president, that would probably be the best thing that he could do." McCain was not the first Republican senator to say so. But he was the first running for president. And in this second run for the White House, McCain would have to do as much as possible to distance himself from an unpopular president.

"Religious freedom does not require Americans to hide their faith from public view."

John McCain

Democrats down the road would portray a McCain presidency as the third term of a Bush White House — "McBush," some opponents called it.

MANY CONTENDERS

This time, McCain faced a crowded field that could split his party into pieces: Mike Huckabee, a former governor of Arkansas and ordained Baptist preacher with a gifted tongue and down-home sense of humor, appealed to Christian conservatives. Mitt Romney, a former governor of Massachusetts, wealthy venture capitalist and onetime CEO for the Olympics, appealed to the business-minded but confronted Christian conservatives wary of his Mormonism. Rudy Giuliani, the former mayor of New York, started the race with a presumptive advantage, a name branded in the aftermath of 9/11, but also appeared to be too liberal for his own party, pro-gun control, pro-abortion rights. Fred Thompson, a prime-time television star and former senator from Tennessee, offered conservatives another option but proved lackluster and even lazy on the campaign trail. Tom Tancredo, a congressman from Colorado, and Sam Brownback, a senator from Kansas, competed for the ultraconservative and anti-immigration reform vote. Duncan Hunter, a congressman from California, courted the military defense-minded. And Ron Paul, an outspoken anti-war obstetrician from Texas who had run as the Libertarian candidate for president 20 years before and was serving his second stint in Congress, cultivated an Internet-based following that generated a lot of attention before the primaries but few votes.

McCain was fortunate that his party's voters were so splintered in the choices they faced because he was still having trouble with the conservative base. In a straw poll of Christian conservative voters convened by the Family Research Council in a Washington hotel ballroom in October 2007, McCain finished dead last of the Republicans who addressed the hall — behind even the "pro-choice" Giuliani. McCain drew 81 votes, Giuliani 107. The favorite of the hall was clearly Huckabee, who collected 1,565 votes. But the sponsors also were permitting online voting, and Romney made a concerted bid for both the hall and online support and carried the day with 1,595 votes.

The Arizonan arrived in this darkened ballroom, where the morning's events opened with a prayer, aware of the hurdle he faced. "I am a conservative Republican and proud of it," McCain said at the Values Voter Summit. With a clear shot at the double-talk he was attributing to his rivals, chiefly Romney and Giuliani, he also told the audience of some 2,000 inside the hall: "I hope you know, I'm not going to con you."

McCain attempted to underscore his core values: "I have been pro-life my entire public career. I believe I am the only major candidate in either party that can make that claim ... I am pro-life because I know what it is like to live without human rights ... That is a personal testament that you need not take on faith. You need only examine my public record to know that I will not change my position." Self-respect is critical, McCain solemnly stated: "I'm not going to trade mine for anyone's vote." He spoke of his days as a prisoner of war and appeared near tears at some turns as he spoke of his captivity in a dimly lit, cement-floored cell where he had learned that "all glory" was not "self-glory" and that he "had to have faith in something greater than myself." He delivered his oft-told tale of a Hanoi prison guard who scratched an image of the cross in the sand before him on Christmas Day, the tale of fellow POW Mike Christian, who had sewn an American flag with a bamboo needle, was beaten for it, picked it up and started sewing again. And he spoke of his own commitment to religious faith and to a conservative Supreme Court.

"Religious freedom does not require Americans to hide their faith from public view," McCain told his audience. And "judges should not legislate from the bench," he said, drawing applause from the audience. "I am proud to have played a role, and a major role, in the confirmation of Judges [Samuel] Alito, [John] Roberts [for the Supreme Court] and many others."

Yet he would have to walk a fine line through some of his beliefs. Unlike Bush, who advocates a constitutional amendment banning gay marriage, McCain opposes such an amendment. And McCain, while asserting during this campaign that adoption belongs to a traditional couple of man and woman, has maintained that this, too, is a matter best left for individual states to decide. "Wisdom suggests that we should be reluctant to change a definition of marriage that has existed for thousands of years," McCain said at that Values Voter Summit. "A mother and a father have complementary roles in the raising of children ... and marriage reinforces" that. McCain, who also believes that the Supreme Court should overturn the 1973 Roe vs. Wade decision that

"Americans are acutely aware of our problems. Their patience is at an end for politicians who value incumbency over principle and for partisanship that is less a contest of ideas than an uncivil brawl over the spoils of power. I want my presidency to be an opportunity — an opportunity to fix what we all know needs to be fixed."

John McCain

made abortion legal, said: "Wisdom suggests that we should be willing to give an unborn child the same chance that our parents gave us."

But this time, when McCain raised his own warrior's credentials, he was no longer campaigning at a time of peace. And he made a simple, moral case for the wars under way in Iraq and Afghanistan and battles against terrorism on other fronts.

"We are involved in a struggle against Islamic extremism," McCain said, and it demands "courage and perseverance on our part. ... We're at a crossroads in this global struggle, and we'll need a president who has the credibility to lead ... and take the right path, even if it means walking a lonely road. ... We have gone to war to defend our security and our values. ... It is a just war, and like all wars, it requires the sacrifice and taking of human life. ... Today, we have another generation of Mike Christians who are over there fighting for someone else's freedom. ... This is our country, fight for it," McCain said in closing. "This is our flag, pick it up. Take it back."

SEEKING AN AIR OF INEVITABILITY

McCain, returning at age 70 for a second run at the White House, had hoped to imbue his candidacy with an air of inevitability. Yet Giuliani had already claimed an early lead among Republicans in opinion polling. McCain, wearing a dark blue sweater under cloudy skies on the banks of the Piscataqua River in Portsmouth, maintained that he alone possessed the experience to serve as president at a time of war: "Americans are acutely aware of our problems. Their patience is at an end for politicians who value incumbency over principle and for partisanship that is less a contest of ideas than an uncivil brawl over the spoils of power. I want my presidency to be an opportunity — an opportunity to fix what we all know needs to be fixed."

Still, if he was intent on charting a new course independent of the White House, he would have to make some amends with the constituency that Bush had corralled, particularly in the president's re-election in 2004: the social conservative base of the Republican Party. In May 2006, McCain, who had called Rev. Jerry Falwell an "agent of intolerance," traveled to Lynchburg, Va., to deliver the commencement address at Falwell's Liberty University.

"When I was a young man, I was quite infatuated with self-expression, and rightly so, because, if memory conveniently serves, I was so much more eloquent, well-informed and wiser than anyone else I knew," McCain told the graduating class at Liberty. "I had opinions on everything, and I was always right. I loved to argue, and I could become understandably belligerent with people who lacked the grace and intelligence to agree with me. With my superior qualities so obvious, it was an intolerable hardship to have to suffer fools gladly. ... It's funny, now, how less self-assured I feel late in life than I did when I lived in perpetual springtime.

"We have our disagreements, we Americans," said McCain, and a big one on this day involved the war in Iraq. "Americans should argue about this war. It has cost the lives of nearly 2,500 of the best of us. It has taken innocent life. It has imposed an enormous financial burden on our economy," he said, but the war against Islamic extremism "is a clash of ideals. ... It is a fight between right and wrong. ... We are insisting that all people have a right to be free, and that right is not subject to the whims and interests and authority of another person, government or culture.

"Let us argue with each other then. By all means, let us argue," McCain said. "Let us exercise our responsibilities as free people. But let us remember, we are not enemies. We are compatriots defending ourselves from a real enemy. We have nothing to fear from each other."

On "Meet the Press" on April 2, 2006, host Tim Russert had asked McCain whether he still saw Falwell as an agent of intolerance. "No, I don't," McCain replied. Yet, in speaking at this or other universities, he said, he was "not embracing all of the tenets." Russert asked: "Are you concerned that people are going to say, 'I see. John McCain tried Straight Talk Express. Maverick. It didn't work in 2000, so now, in 2008, he's going to become a conventional, typical politician, reaching out to people

In March 2008, former First Lady Nancy Reagan, with McCain at her home in Bel Air, Calif., said that she and President Reagan were impressed by the courage McCain showed as a prisoner of war in Vietnam. She also endorsed him.

that he called agents of intolerance, voting for tax cuts he opposed, to make himself more appealing to the hard-core Republican base.'"

"I think most people will judge my record exactly for what it is, where I take positions that I stand for and I believe in," McCain replied. "I don't think that my position on immigration is exactly pleasing to the far right base. I will continue to take positions that I believe in and I stand for. And I recognize that a lot of my credibility is based on that."

The Democratic National Committee gladly jumped in, declaring that McCain had taken "the Doubletalk Express for a spin." Karen Finney, a DNC spokeswoman,

Following page
In March 2008, McCain prepares to take off in a Black Hawk from an air base in Iraq. He made an unexpected visit and talked with Iraqi and U.S. diplomatic and military officials.

citing another term that McCain had once used for Falwell, said: "This morning, John McCain embraced a man he once called an 'evil influence' on the Republican Party. McCain has changed his position so many times that Americans can't know where he stands on anything."

McCain organized an exploratory campaign for president later that year, after Democrats reclaimed the House and Senate in midterm elections and after Rumsfeld resigned. In a speech to a conservative organization, GOPAC, McCain warned that Republicans had betrayed the principles that put them in office. "We lost our principles and our majority," said McCain, blaming the party for a proliferation of "pork-barrel" spending and a swollen government "in the false hope that we could bribe the public into keeping us in office. ... There is no way to recover our majority without recovering our principles first."

Still, if the prosecution of an unpopular war also had contributed to the GOP's loss of control of Congress, McCain maintained that the war in Iraq was not negotiable. On Jan. 10, 2007, McCain said in an interview with CNN's Larry King: "I would much rather lose a campaign than lose a war."

At the time, any conventional handicapping of the 2008 presidential election suggested that the Democrats might nominate Sen. Hillary Clinton of New York for president. She, like McCain, had voted for the authorization of military force in Iraq, though she, too, had grown critical of the conduct of the war. At the time, McCain did not appear to be his party's leading candidate for president. A Washington Post-ABC News Poll on Jan. 19, 2007, found that 34 percent of the Republicans surveyed favored Giuliani, 27 percent McCain. And Giuliani's margin would grow to 30 percentage points by some measures in the months ahead. Among Democrats at the time, Clinton was the runaway favorite. And at the time, there appeared to be little prospect that Sen. Barack Obama, the junior senator from Illinois, who hadn't even been a member of the Senate when the war vote was taken but said at the time that he would have opposed it, would become the Democratic Party's presidential nominee. In retrospect, it's also noteworthy that the January 2007 Post-ABC poll found this in a hypothetical matchup: Obama 47 percent, McCain 45 percent.

The day after clinching the Republican nomination, McCain appeared in the Rose Garden with President George W. Bush in March 2008. Bush credited McCain with "incredible courage and strength of character and perseverance in order to get to this moment."

"We took a pretty good pounding for the last few weeks on immigration, and it had an effect. But McCain is not going to pander his way to the nomination."

Mark Salter, McCain adviser

Through the spring of 2007, the war in Iraq overshadowed everything else in a presidential campaign already under way. And McCain was making an early bid to build some support in a state he had bypassed during the first tour of his "Straight Talk Express." "We used to beg and cajole and bribe people to come ride with us," McCain joked in Iowa in March 2007, sitting in a plush new campaign bus surrounded by national and local reporters. He was drawing capacity crowds from Ames to Mason City and Cedar Falls. He was trailing Giuliani by 30 points in recent polls. And now, rather than "poking evangelical Christians in the eye as he did last time," as the Chicago Tribune's Jill Zuckman put it, he was "courting them and appealing to conservatives who view him with suspicion for his positions on immigration and campaign financing." And now, in Iowa, he was speaking of the virtues of ethanol. McCain even joked: "I drink a glass of ethanol every morning with [Iowa Sen.] Chuck Grassley for breakfast."

In the first of many crowded Republican candidate debates, in early May 2007, at the Ronald Reagan Presidential Library and Museum in Simi Valley, Calif., Nancy Reagan sat in the front row of an encounter in which McCain and most of his rivals vied for the mantle of the Reagan Republican. Mitt Romney had suggested that the hunt for Al Qaeda leader Osama bin Laden was not worth billions of dollars, but he vowed in this debate that, "He is going to pay, and he will die." McCain, who had previously derided Romney's words as naive, raised the stakes at this televised faceoff: "We will do whatever is necessary," McCain said of bin Laden. "We will track him down. We will catch him. We will bring him to justice, and I will follow him to the gates of hell."

McCain had gained somewhat on Giuliani among Republicans, according to the latest Quinnipiac University poll showing Giuliani drawing 27 percent of the Republicans surveyed, McCain 19 percent and Fred Thompson, a fixture of television's "Law & Order," at 14 percent — even though Thompson was not even a candidate at the time. Conservatives were still casting about for an alternative to the pro-choice Giuliani and the party-bucking McCain, and Romney was not registering much support nationally in the early days of the campaign.

Yet in New Hampshire, which had been key for McCain before, Romney was making great strides. Romney was raising a lot of money — $21 million in the first quarter of that year — and the latest polls in both the early caucus and primary states were favorable for him: The Des Moines Register found Romney leading in Iowa in late May 2007, and a Zogby poll in New Hampshire found Romney much stronger than either McCain or Giuliani. The McCain campaign's spokesman at the time was registering a question about Romney that McCain would later level at Obama. "The question for voters is: Does a one-term governor from Massachusetts have the foreign policy experience necessary to deal with the challenges of today's world?" Brian Jones said.

CAMPAIGN OVERHAUL

By Independence Day of 2007, McCain's big-spending campaign was running aground. He had raised less during the second quarter of the year, $11.2 million, than he had during the first quarter, about $12.5 million, and he had just $2 million left in the bank. His campaign announced widespread layoffs, the campaign manager staying on without pay. McCain had campaigned as a front-runner, with an extensive and expensive staff and a raft of consultants. But his stance on the war and his advocacy of an immigration reform unpopular within his party were taking a toll. "We took a pretty good pounding for the last few weeks on immigration, and it had an effect," said Mark Salter, a senior McCain adviser in the Senate who had co-authored the senator's books, "Faith of My Fathers" and "Worth the Fighting For." "But McCain is not going to pander his way to the nomination."

McCain went to Iraq, to spend the 4th of July with troops. And later that month, McCain again turned to the place he had learned to love most: New Hampshire. McCain dropped his campaign manager and chief strategist and traveled to Concord, where everyone wanted to know how he might fight his way out of this hole. "We go to the town hall meetings, we fix our financial difficulties and we win," McCain said. "We'll win almost the same way we won in 2000." Asked whether anything might persuade him to drop out, he replied: "Contracting a fatal disease."

McCain also confronted the issues that had become problematic for him with his own party's base as well as the independent voters he had counted on in 2000: "My

In Miami, U.S. Navy veteran Joe Martory waits for John McCain to speak in January 2008.

position on immigration was obviously not helpful with the Republican base. My position on the war in Iraq is at least not helpful with independents. But I take responsibility for my positions."

McCain waged a ground war in the town halls of New Hampshire, and an air war with new TV ads underscoring his story as a prisoner of war and his credentials for the war on terrorism. Media adviser Mark McKinnon told the Tribune's Zuckman: "John McCain knows the horrors of war; he's seen the face of evil."

The candidate also started leveling more criticism at his rivals, Romney and Giuliani: "Tough talk or managerial successes in the private sector aren't adequate assurance that their authors have the experience or qualities necessary for such a singular responsibility," he said in New York in late September 2007.

In the chill of New Hampshire's winter, as McCain maintained that he was starting "to feel the enthusiasm" that he had found in 2000, McCain found some warmth inside a restaurant in Colebrook one morning. Samuel Bird, a retired schoolteacher and independent voter at breakfast in Howard's Restaurant, said that he and his wife were angry with the Bush administration and planned to vote in the Democratic primary. He had always liked McCain but viewed him differently now: "The feeling I get is he's a spokesman for Bush in a lot of ways," Bird told the Tribune. "He was so much his own man a couple years ago." And then Bird asked the candidate: "What happened to the maverick? It used to be Republican, Democrat, and what John McCain said."

"I'm still the maverick," McCain replied at that restaurant. "I'm too old to change."

Toward the end of the year, the stumbling American economy was starting to supplant the war as a primary concern among voters, and Huckabee, the amiable Baptist preacher from Arkansas, was gaining ground in Iowa. In New Hampshire, the iconic Union Leader of Manchester had endorsed McCain and suggested that "the more Romney speaks, the less believable he becomes." And a poll conducted by The Boston Globe at year's end portrayed Romney and McCain in a statistical tie there.

McCain offered an admission about economics that opponents would make him pay for down the road, explaining near the close of the New Hampshire campaign: "The issue of economics is something that I've never really understood as well as I should. I understand the basics, the fundamentals, the vision, all that kind of stuff." It was his way of suggesting that, as president, he would call on strong advisers. But critics would seize on that confession. And later, one of McCain's closest advisers on economic matters, former Sen. Phil Gramm of Texas, would quit the campaign after claiming that Americans are "a nation of whiners" about the economy — offering opponents a one-two punch against McCain on this front.

When the premier party caucuses and primaries

Following page
In Chicago, Sen. Joe Lieberman, an Independent, campaigns with McCain at the National Restaurant Association convention in May 2008. Lieberman, a former Democrat, endorsed McCain.

"John McCain knows the horrors of war; he's seen the face of evil."

Mark McKinnon, McCain media adviser

arrived, in January 2008, Huckabee claimed Iowa's Republicans, and McCain won New Hampshire: With 37 percent of the votes in the GOP primary, McCain led Romney by 5 points. And already, in both Iowa and New Hampshire, the once-vaunted star of the Republican pack, Giuliani, was fading away. He placed fourth in New Hampshire and sixth in Iowa. Romney would prevail in Michigan, where his father had been governor. Yet Romney did not run away with the state on Jan. 15, claiming 39 percent of the GOP vote. McCain claimed 30 percent. And again Giuliani was flailing: sixth.

By the time the Republicans reached Florida, on Jan. 29, a once-crowded party primary was thinning out rapidly. With an eleventh-hour nod from the Sunshine State's popular Republican governor, Charlie Crist, McCain claimed 36 percent of the vote in Florida's GOP contest, Romney 31 percent. And Giuliani, who by this point had staked all of his struggling campaign's hopes on the state, finished a distant third, with 15 percent. By the following morning, Giuliani was bowing out and endorsing McCain.

For McCain, the comeback only added to a legend he had started writing eight years before. "As Chairman Mao says, it's always darkest before it's totally black," McCain said of his rise and fall and rise again. "I had no illusions of how tough it was," he said, "but I never thought of it in terms of, 'Well, you're basically through.'" McCain believed his trip to Iraq at the nadir of his campaign had kept him in the race. He had given an emotional address there and shaken the hands of young men and women serving. He also realized he had allowed his campaign to spend with the same license for which he had often criticized the government. He said the town halls of New Hampshire had allowed him to reconnect with voters. And he wasn't backing down on the war. At a debate in New Hampshire, a woman told the candidate about her brother, 1st Lt. Michael Joseph Cleary, killed in action in Iraq eight days before he was supposed to come home. She pleaded with the candidates to say what they would do to "bring this conflict to a point at which we can safely bring our troops home." McCain rose from his stool and said: "This war was very badly managed for a long time, and Americans have made great sacrifices, some of which were unnecessary because of this mismanagement. ... I believe we have a strategy which can succeed, so that the sacrifice of your brother would not be in vain. ... I believe if we fail, it will become a center of terrorism, and we will ask more young Americans to sacrifice, as your brother did."

The senator had embarked on a "No Surrender Tour," traveling from Iowa to New Hampshire to South Carolina and visiting Veterans of Foreign Wars and American Legion halls, making the case for the war with a band of POW friends. He had, in fact, staked his campaign on the course of the war.

But something else was happening as well: American military casualties were subsiding in Iraq, and Bush and supporters were contending that the "surge" of U.S. forces was working. The White House also was starting to talk about scaling back forces to pre-surge levels. Sen. Lindsey Graham, a South Carolina Republican who has campaigned hard for McCain and is one of his best friends in the Senate, told the Tribune's Zuckman: "If the surge had failed, nobody could have resurrected this campaign."

On Feb. 5, Super Tuesday, it was virtually over for the Republicans. McCain's advantage was insurmountable, though Huckabee would remain an amiable sole foil to McCain in the primaries that followed — explaining that he had "majored in miracles," not math — until McCain actually clinched the delegates needed for the party's nomination.

McCain, who had sought and fallen short of his party's presidential nomination eight years before, formally clinched it on March 4, 2008, with wins in Ohio, Texas, Rhode Island and Vermont. "I understand the responsibilities I incur with this nomination, and I give you my word, I will not evade or slight a single one," McCain said in Dallas. "Our campaign must be and will be more than another tired debate of false promises, empty sound bites and useless arguments from the past that address not a single American's concerns for their family's security."

He insisted that he would present voters with a candidate who puts "principles" ahead of "platitudes." He repeated some of the words he had delivered at Liberty University two years earlier: "Their patience is at an end for politicians who value ambition over principle, and for partisanship that is less a contest of ideas than an uncivil brawl over the spoils of power."

The next morning, a jubilant McCain appeared in the Rose Garden of the White House, standing next to the man with whom he had shared a most "uncivil brawl" in 2000. Bush, crediting McCain with "incredible courage and strength of character and perseverance in order to get to this moment," suggested that that's what

Americans are looking for in a president. McCain, collecting the endorsement of an erstwhile enemy from whom he still would seek to distance himself in the campaign ahead, said of Bush: "I hope that he will campaign for me as much as is keeping with his busy schedule." Bush, asked whether he might hurt McCain more than he might help him, replied: "Look ... if my showing up and endorsing him helps him, or if I'm against him and it helps him — either way, I want him to win. ... If he wants my pretty face standing by his side at one of these rallies, I'll be glad to show up."

This wouldn't be all the peacemaking McCain would face in the months ahead. The candidate who had leveled warlike words at his Republican rival in the primaries of 2000 also had insisted that he would make the toughest opponent for Democrat Al Gore — "I'm gonna beat Al Gore like a drum," McCain had said then. But this time, in courting the middle-of-the-road voter in pursuit of the White House, that so-called "McCain Majority," he would face an opponent, Sen. Obama, attempting to appeal to some of the same voters, the independent-minded, swing voters who had bolstered McCain's primary campaigns. Midsummer, McCain was attempting to leaven his own criticism for Obama over the war with the civility he hoped to make a hallmark of his long-sought nomination for the presidency.

PRAISE FOR HIS OPPONENT

McCain, appearing at an NAACP meeting in July and addressing a constituency likely to support the first African-American nominee of a major party by an overwhelming margin in November, told his audience: "Whatever the outcome in November, Sen. Obama has achieved a great thing, for himself and for his country, and I thank him for it. ... Don't tell him I said this, but he is an impressive fellow in many ways."

Yet McCain would take the debate to his rival, as he always had. When Obama argued that the United States was fighting the wrong war in Iraq and that U.S. forces should be shifted to Afghanistan, McCain dismissed his rival at one of his own town hall rallies in New Mexico for suddenly "talking tough" about war. And when Obama made a summer tour of war fronts in Afghanistan and Iraq, McCain maintained that it was the success of the "surge" in U.S. forces, which he had supported and Obama had opposed, that made the Iraq visit possible. "He's been completely wrong on the issue," McCain said of Obama, dismissing his rival as "someone who has no military experience whatsoever."

McCain would attempt to accentuate an experience gap between himself and Obama. After Obama finished a summer tour of Europe, where he drew large and adoring crowds, the McCain campaign aired a television ad calling Obama "the biggest celebrity in the world." The ad derisively likened Obama's public appeal to that of singer Britney Spears and socialite Paris Hilton. This pointed ad, auguring a potentially volatile fall campaign, asked this about McCain's rival for the presidency: "Is he ready to lead?"

While Obama toured Iraq, McCain made an appearance on the waterfront lawn of former President George H.W. Bush's family compound in Kennebunkport, Maine, standing alongside a commander in chief who had won his own war, the Persian Gulf War that forced Saddam Hussein out of Kuwait, in 1991. "The commander in chief doesn't get a learning curve. ... I will bring to the job many years of military and political experience," McCain had said before. "I won't bluster, and I won't make idle threats, but understand this, when I am the commander in chief, there will be no place the terrorists can run and nowhere they can hide."

Yet now, with Obama promising to bring U.S. troops home within 16 months of his election as president, McCain was setting his own rough timeline. This would be a much closer horizon than the troop deployment of "100 years" McCain had casually mentioned during his party's primary contest. In an interview aired by NBC "Nightly News" on July 24, McCain asserted: "I'm sure that by the end of my first term as president we will be largely out of there." And in an interview the next day, aired on CNN, McCain acknowledged this of the 16-month timeframe: "I think it's a pretty good timetable, as we should [have our] horizons for withdrawal. But they have to be based on conditions on the ground."

Following page
John McCain (from left front), Cindy, daughter Meghan and Florida Gov. Charlie Crist tour Everglades Safari Park in June 2008.

EVERGLADES Safari

9 *McCain, The Man: "Somebody who tells it like it is"*

DAYS BEFORE JOHN MCCAIN faced the judgment of the ornery voters of New Hampshire in January 2008, Bob Schieffer, host of CBS News' "Face the Nation," welcomed a candidate who had made an extraordinary comeback. Polls portrayed McCain as being on the verge of winning New Hampshire, after his campaign had nearly gone bust months before. "With us is Sen. John McCain, who is hot, hot, hot, according to these latest polls," Schieffer told his viewers. "He has now pulled into a lead, a small one but a lead, over Mitt Romney." Turning toward his guest, the amiable Schieffer said: "I must say, Senator, six weeks ago I never would have thought that."

"Bob," McCain replied with a smile, "that just shows that you're not very bright or prescient." And the two laughed.

It was a joke in the tradition of a deep repertoire of McCain's quick, sometimes biting barbs. But it was a reflection, nonetheless, of McCain's capacity for letting others around him not-so-subtly know just who he thinks might know best in any given situation. He has a proclivity, he has allowed of himself, toward a certain "irremediable" trait — the "wiseass," as he has put it. As McCain told the graduating class of Liberty University in 2006, when he was a younger man, he was "quite infatuated with self-expression, and rightly so, because, if memory conveniently serves, I was so much more eloquent, well-informed and wiser than anyone else I knew." He had "opinions on everything," he told the graduates, was "always right" and "could become understandably belligerent with people who lacked the grace and intelligence to agree with me." As his prep-school yearbook from Episcopal High had it: "His magnetic personality has won for him many life-long

McCain is known for an explosive temper, but also for laughing at his own jokes and poking fun at himself.

friends. But, as magnets must also repel, some have found him hard to get along with."

McCain's occasionally explosive temper is no secret in the halls of the Senate. Elizabeth Drew, in "Citizen McCain," quotes "one senator," also an admirer, as saying, "Dealing with John is kind of like dancing with a cactus." Drew has written that McCain "does explode on occasion, but he also knows how and when to keep his temper under control. ... But McCain's temper is famous in large part because he's famous and in part because he has some dedicated enemies in the Senate."

McCain also enjoys laughing at his own jokes, as he did when MSNBC's Joe Scarborough asked him whether he worried that Bob Barr, the Libertarian Party candidate for president in 2008, might peel away some of McCain's support in November. "I'm confident that at the end of the day ... Republicans and Democrats and independents and Libertarians and vegetarians will vote for me," replied McCain, with a chuckle over his own remark.

"He's got a great sense of humor. It's very playful, but it can be dark," said Mike Murphy, a media adviser who served McCain in the 2000 campaign. "He's had a lifetime of dealing with hard reality ... the prison, politics. ... He doesn't live in an ivory tower."

McCain's propensity for confession, both in his self-excavating memoirs and in public appearances, bespeaks a seemingly endlessly unfulfilled desire to set the record straight about himself. It appears to be an effort to explain, both to himself and to others, his reputation for rebelliousness in the context of a larger journey of learning. He has learned, he insists, the meaning of "glory." It involves serving a cause greater than oneself, as he has defined it. And, as he has admitted to many audiences — including one at a campaign stop in March at the airfield in Mississippi that bears his family's name and where he trained to fly as a war pilot — he has been "an imperfect servant of my country."

His relentless pursuit of candor has even led him to return to the scene of a campaign past, as he did in South Carolina, in 2000, and admit that he had refrained from telling the whole truth about his views on the Confederate flag. He had compromised his own values, he confessed in a public apology that was completely of his own choosing, required only by his own desire to set the record right for perhaps another go-round. His relentless, years-long pursuit of campaign finance reform followed his own humiliating entanglement in the web of

Supporters cheer as McCain arrives for a rally in Keene, N.H., in January 2008.

McCAIN

DividedWeFail

McCain laughs with the media as he travels between Ames and Iowa Falls, Iowa, on the "Straight Talk Express" bus in March 2007.

Washington money and influence as a new senator. He had shown "poor judgment" and admitted it.

He has served his country also as an employee of the government, for most of his life: Since graduation from the U.S. Naval Academy in 1958, McCain has spent little more than a year in the private sector, with a stint in public relations for his wife's beer distributorship in Phoenix. McCain retired from the Navy in 1981 only to win election to Congress in November 1982 — a career in public service spanning nearly 50 years.

Much of McCain's career — both his first in the military and his second in politics — has centered on a certain redemption. At war, in Vietnam, he seized an opportunity to recast an image of rowdiness that could be getting in the way of his naval career, to regain a career track that, like his father's and grandfather's before him, had started in the halls of the Naval Academy. In government, on Capitol Hill, he forged the image of a maverick beholden to not even his own party or president and embraced a persona that would serve him well in one presidential campaign and even better in the next. It is, one friend suggests, a "matter of honor" with McCain.

Murphy, who served McCain in his first campaign for president but was independent of any candidate in the second, explains the return to South Carolina to speak out about the flag: "It became a question of honor to him, and he was going to clear that account. ... I think he just feels that when he has done something that he thought in hindsight was a mistake, he has a need, which I think is kind of commendable, to confess that. He is more Catholic than he knows. Part of the penance of making a mistake is to acknowledge it and confess it. It's part of what makes McCain McCain. To him, nothing is more important than honor."

McCain also has presented two faces to the public in his campaigns. The hard-charging campaign that McCain waged against George Bush in 2000 had a distinctly different flavor than the one he was waging against Barack Obama in 2008. McCain fought the political equivalent of a death match with Bush. He was conducting, by comparison, a parlor debate with Obama. McCain has called his rival an "impressive fellow."

McCain, who had been the star candidate of the 2000 campaign, the onetime prisoner of war who was roaming

"He's got a great sense of humor. It's very playful, but it can be dark. He's had a lifetime of dealing with hard reality... the prison, politics. ... He doesn't live in an ivory tower."

Mike Murphy, McCain media adviser

the countryside in a campaign bus open to all, was confronting, in 2008, a rival with considerable star power of his own, the first African-American nominee of a major political party and an eloquent speaker who had electrified crowds with his call for change. "He is very eloquent, and he has motivated many, many millions of people," McCain allowed about his opponent in an appearance on MSNBC in July. "I respect him and admire him. There are just stark differences. And I think the American people will make a judgment at the end of the day on who's best to keep America prosperous and safe, and I think I can prevail there."

"McCain is now the official candidate of the Republican Party," Murphy explains, and with that comes an obligation for a certain gravitas. McCain is at his best on the high road, his former adviser suggests. McCain would be better-served if attacks on Obama were left to his surrogates, the media adviser said, yet McCain also would be better-served if his campaign simply got out of his way more often. "Some of the spirit of 2000 would help him now," said Murphy, who refrained from joining any campaign in 2008 because he had served both McCain and Mitt Romney, one of McCain's rivals in the latest primaries. McCain's advisers have shielded him more from the press this time around, in Murphy's view, and that has not helped. "The more he uses his authentic self the better, but his campaign has gotten in the way."

The 2000 campaign was "just kind of a different campaign," Murphy said. "There wasn't as much orthodoxy. We thought the way to win was to amplify — to let McCain be McCain. I think this campaign is more cautious. ... I think he has lost some of that spark, and if he gets that back, that will help him in the stretch."

Orson Swindle, whom McCain first met as a fellow prisoner of war in Hanoi, has remained a friend through the years. Swindle retired from the Marine Corps in 1979 as a lieutenant colonel and served the Reagan administration in the Commerce Department. He has campaigned for McCain in 2000 and in 2008. If there is a difference between this campaign and the past one, Swindle said, it is only the circumstances of the race.

"John McCain is John McCain. He hasn't changed a hell of a lot," said Swindle, asked about the volatile campaign against Bush in 2000 and the relatively civil contest McCain was waging with Obama in 2008. "As far as his remarks about Barack Obama, he states fact. Barack Obama is an impressive guy. ... He has also drawn just profound distinctions between himself and Barack Obama. ... You couldn't find a greater difference," Swindle said with a certain partisanship. "One has a world of experience, and the other could not be more naive or have less experience.

"If you really want leadership and not a rock star, the choice is obvious," McCain's longtime friend suggested. "We might be the 'American Idol' generation, but this is serious business, and we face a very dangerous and challenging world. One man in this race has demonstrated remarkable courage."

The first campaign also was waged at a time of peace, the second at a time of war. And McCain made a fateful decision early in his successful pursuit of the GOP's nomination to tie himself to what was becoming an unpopular war — "a courageous" decision, in Murphy's view. "When the war was popular, he took the unpopular position of criticizing [Defense Secretary] Rumsfeld, and then when the war became unpopular, he continued to defend it. He has run [with] the principled decision, but never the popular one, on the war. ... It will be a great test to see if he is rewarded. People say they want that in a president, somebody who tells it like it is and puts the country first. Well, we're going to find out."

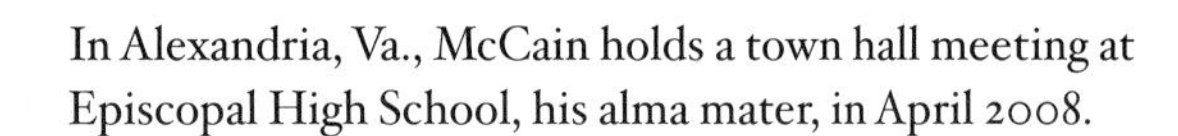

In Alexandria, Va., McCain holds a town hall meeting at Episcopal High School, his alma mater, in April 2008.

Following pages
McCain makes an appearance at a Westgate Mall market in Bethlehem, Pa., in July 2008.

In Miami's Little Havana neighborhood, the crowd applauds McCain in May 2008 after he toured a building dedicated in honor of political prisoners held in Cuba.

EXIT
WITH US!

ACCION CUBANA
SEGURIDAD NACIONAL PARA U.S.A. CON JOHN McCAIN

9 *On the Issues*

SEN. JOHN MCCAIN has charted his own course on many issues. He has bucked his party's presidents on taxation but has stood solidly with President Bush on the "surge" of U.S. forces in Iraq. He hews to his party's line against abortion and has called on the Supreme Court to overturn Roe vs. Wade, but he opposes a constitutional amendment banning abortion. He has been a champion of campaign finance reform, over the objections of party leaders, and a sponsor of immigration reform, alienating his party's conservative base.

McCain's position

THE WAR IN IRAQ

Sen. John McCain was among the members of Congress who, in October 2002, supported the use of U.S. military force against Iraq. McCain became a critic of the early conduct of the war, ultimately voicing a loss of confidence in Defense Secretary Donald Rumsfeld. McCain supported the "surge" in forces President Bush ordered in January 2007 and credits it with making Iraq more secure. He maintains that U.S. forces must remain there until Iraq can defend itself, and has called a decades-long commitment of U.S. forces there acceptable so long as Americans aren't suffering casualties.

Obama's position

Like no other, this was the issue that propelled Obama through the early months of a primary campaign where many of the leading candidates had voted to support an invasion. As he prepared to run for the U.S. Senate in 2004, Obama had given a speech in Chicago in 2002 against the invasion. He constantly reminded activists of it as he campaigned in Iowa and New Hampshire. Obama was critical of the "surge" that some have credited with making Iraq more secure. He has called for a 16-month timetable for withdrawal of combat troops, which he has said he would start as soon as taking office.

THE WAR ON TERROR

The terrorist attacks of Sept. 11, 2001, "represented more than a failure of intelligence," McCain says. They underscored a failure of national policy in the face of a growing global network of terrorism. He pushed for and supported the 9/11 Commission that investigated the attacks. McCain maintains a commitment to a war against "violent Islamic extremists" on all fronts "using all instruments of national power." This includes engagement with enemies "on the battlefield of ideas." McCain has pledged to hunt down Osama bin Laden — "to the gates of hell" if necessary.

Obama has called for a clear set of federal regulations for chemical plants that would enhance security and safety training. He has also called for improved tracking of spent fuel rods from nuclear power plants. Seeking to keep drinking water safe, Obama has called for upgrades in monitoring and security efforts. He believes the central front on the war against terrorism is Afghanistan, not Iraq.

THE MILITARY

McCain supports an enlargement of the U.S. military "to meet new challenges to our security." He supports an increase in deployment of U.S. forces in Afghanistan. The military also must be funded under the routine budget of the federal government, he believes, as opposed to the repeated emergency appropriations that have financed the wars in Iraq and Afghanistan. To guard against the threats of hostile nations, he supports the creation of new missile defenses such as the missile battery in Poland and radar network in the Czech Republic that the Bush administration has promoted.

Obama maintains that the nation's military is a "20th Century structure" despite facing "21st Century problems." He believes such things as special operations forces, civil affairs and information operations must be built up. He supports plans to increase the size of the Army by 65,000 soldiers and the Marines by 27,000 troops. Obama has committed to a review of each major defense program, while also maintaining that "unparalleled airpower" remains essential. He supports missile defense, as long as it is developed in a way that is "pragmatic and cost-effective."

McCain's position

TAXES

McCain opposed the first round of Bush tax cuts as too heavily weighted toward the wealthy but supported an acceleration of the cuts in 2003 and the final tax bill in 2006. He also backs a continuation of the Bush tax cuts. He proposes a permanent repeal of the Alternative Minimum Tax and promises to cut taxes for the middle class and corporations. He has promised to avert new taxes if he is elected president and would like to see a 60 percent vote requirement in Congress for any new taxes. He supports a ban on Internet taxes. And he has pledged to pursue a "simpler" alternative to the existing federal income tax.

Obama's position

Obama has called for tax relief for 150 million workers through a "Making Work Pay" tax credit of up to $500 per person, or $1,000 per working family. His campaign says the tax credit would completely eliminate income taxes for 10 million Americans. He would also eliminate income taxes for seniors making less than $50,000 a year. Obama wants the Bush administration's tax cuts for those who make more than $250,000 a year eliminated and would extend and index the Alternative Minimum Tax patch, something that keeps it from applying to even more taxpayers than it already does.

SPENDING

McCain pledges to ban the earmarks that enable members of Congress to slip spending for special projects back home into federal spending bills. He vows to "make their authors famous," promising presidential vetoes of "pork-barrel" spending. He has proposed a one-year halt in the increase of "discretionary" federal spending to make a "top-to-bottom review" of all federal programs. Facing a near-record federal budget deficit, in which government spending now exceeds revenue by more than $400 billion a year, McCain says he "will not leave office without balancing the federal budget." He has promised a balanced budget by 2013.

Obama has proposed billions in spending to create jobs and enhance government programs to help the less fortunate. He plans to fund those by ending the Iraq War, eliminating corporate tax breaks and raising taxes on those with higher incomes. Obama says he is a big believer in pay-as-you-go budgeting rules that require new spending initiatives or tax changes to be paid for by cuts to other programs or new revenue. He has pushed for more disclosure and transparency for earmarks in the federal budget. Obama urges the elimination of subsidies for oil and gas companies and has pledged to "tackle wasteful spending in the Medicare program."

GAS PRICES

The senator has supported a summer "holiday" from the federal gas tax, suggesting that holding the 18.4-cents-per-gallon tax in abeyance from Memorial Day to Labor Day could help ease the burden on consumers from prices that soared to over $4 per gallon this summer. He has pledged to stop filling the federal Strategic Petroleum Reserve to ease pressure on oil prices. He has proposed lifting a longtime federal ban against oil drilling on the Outer Continental Shelf, to make more oil available. He has proposed to eliminate policies that contribute to higher transportation and food costs — including a federal subsidy for the production of ethanol.

Although the gas tax "holiday" idea was quickly endorsed by Sen. Hillary Clinton, who was desperately trying to slow Obama's progress in winning the nomination, Obama objected, calling the idea a "gimmick," even though it was popular with many voters facing surging pump prices. In early August, Obama altered his position on tapping the nation's Strategic Petroleum Reserve to help relieve gas prices. That move came just days after Obama softened his position on the expansion of oil drilling along the nation's coastline.

McCain's position	*Obama's position*
ENERGY In addition to permitting oil and natural gas exploration and production on the Outer Continental Shelf, McCain proposes reducing dependence on foreign oil. He suggests a "Clean Car Challenge" for American automakers: Offering a $5,000 tax credit for purchases of "zero carbon emission" cars and encouraging automakers to be first to market with such vehicles. He proposes a $300 million federal prize for the manufacturer of a significantly improved car battery. He supports the advancement of clean coal in power generation and vows to put the country on track toward building 45 new nuclear power plants by 2030.	Obama has pledged to create 5 million new jobs by investing $150 billion over the next decade to build cleaner energy generation. He has called for a national goal within 10 years of saving more oil than is now imported from the Middle East and Venezuela combined. He wants to see 1 million plug-in hybrid cars capable of getting up to 150 miles per gallon on the road by 2015. Obama wants to ensure that 10 percent of electricity comes from renewable sources by 2012, with a full quarter of it coming from those sources by 2025.
SOCIAL SECURITY McCain maintains that any solution to the economic imbalance in the Social Security system must be a bipartisan plan. And he has pledged that he "will not leave office without fixing the problems that threaten our future prosperity." He has supported President Bush's proposal for personal retirement savings plans as a supplement to the long-standing federal payroll tax deductions financing Social Security. McCain has maintained that he opposes any increase in the payroll tax to fix Social Security but has said that, in the spirit of bipartisan negotiations, "There is nothing that's off the table. I have my positions, and I'll articulate them."	Obama supports making some with higher incomes pay more in Social Security taxes, specifically those making more than $250,000 annually, or roughly the top 3 percent of income earners. The 6.2 percent payroll tax is now applied to wages up to $102,000 a year. Obama's plan would not increase the tax on wages between that amount and $250,000.
HOUSING In the face of a home mortgage foreclosure crisis, McCain has proposed a "HOME Plan" to enable "deserving" families "to trade a burdensome mortgage" for a loan more reflective of their home's value. Those who secured non-conventional mortgages after 2005 and cannot meet the payments but are credit-worthy could apply for a new 30-year fixed-rate mortgage. He also would form a Department of Justice task force to investigate criminal wrongdoing in the mortgage industry. McCain, calling the estate tax a "death tax," supports raising its exemption from taxation to estates valued at up to $10 million while cutting the tax rate.	Citing his experience with the issue in Chicago, Obama has pledged to crack down on mortgage fraud. He would create a "Universal Mortgage Credit" for homeowners who do not itemize on their tax returns. For home buyers, he wants to create a Homeowner Obligation Made Explicit score, which would provide potential borrowers with a simplified, standardized metric to help compare various mortgage products and understand the full cost of a loan.

McCain's position

Obama's position

HEALTH CARE

McCain: He opposes a new government-financed system of health care for the 47 million Americans who are uninsured, and voted against extending prescription drug benefits to Medicare patients. He hopes instead to make private health insurance more affordable. He supports relief in the tax code, including a tax credit of $2,500 for individuals and $5,000 for families, to offset the cost of private health insurance for those not covered by their employers. He wants health insurance to be portable from job to job. He proposes expanding the benefits of Health Savings Accounts that enable people to set aside money tax-free for health care.

Obama: Obama would make available a new national health plan to all Americans, including the self-employed and small businesses. He often tells audiences that they will be able to buy affordable health coverage that is similar to the plan available to members of Congress. Under his plan, eligibility would be guaranteed and subsidies would be available for those who do not qualify for Medicaid. Although coverage for children would be required, he stops short of universal coverage.

EDUCATION

McCain: The senator has supported the No Child Left Behind legislation of the Bush administration, which requires annual testing in public schools to ensure "adequate yearly progress" is being made. "This age of honest reporting" has exposed which schools are succeeding and which ones are failing, he believes. In addition, he says, any child in a school that fails to improve should be able to change schools. And he wants to empower parents to send their children to private schools if public schools are insufficient. A supporter of school choice, he has backed federal tuition vouchers to assist parents.

Obama: The senator has called for a "Zero to Five" plan that would provide support to children and parents, stressing early care and education for infants. He would expand Early Head Start and Head Start and pledges to provide affordable, high-quality child care for working families. Obama often talks about reforming the federal No Child Left Behind program and providing more school funding. He has promised to do more to recruit, prepare, retain and reward teachers. Although he sends his children to a private school, he opposes vouchers for those who select to send their kids to private schools.

IMMIGRATION

McCain: The Republican senator, along with Democratic co-sponsors in the Senate, has supported "comprehensive immigration reform." This includes not only a strengthening of borders, but also offering those who qualify, among an estimated 12 million or more illegal immigrants already in the U.S., a path toward legal residence and potential citizenship. "As president," McCain promises, "I will secure the border." In addition, he would enable workers who entered the U.S. illegally but have found jobs, learned English and avoided further criminal wrongdoing to seek a path to citizenship. America will always be that "shining city upon a hill," McCain says.

Obama: Obama says he wants to "preserve the integrity of our borders" and supports additional personnel, infrastructure and technology at the border and ports of entry. He would work to remove incentives to illegally enter the country by cracking down on employers who hire undocumented immigrants. He also supports a system that allows undocumented immigrants in good standing to pay a fine, learn English and then "go to the back of the line" for the opportunity to become citizens. By working to promote economic development in Mexico, he believes, illegal immigration could be reduced.

McCain's position	*Obama's position*
CLIMATE CHANGE McCain acknowledges the impact of man-made emissions on global warming. He believes that emissions can be curbed with a market-based system of "caps and trades." He proposes setting limits on greenhouse gas emissions and then allowing businesses to buy and sell rights to emit pollutants. Any company that could reduce its own emissions could sell emissions rights to others. He proposes a timetable for reducing emissions of greenhouse gases in the United States by more than half: Returning emissions to their 2005 levels by 2012, and taking emissions back to 1990 levels by 2050. This would amount to a 66 percent reduction, he says.	Obama has proposed an economy-wide cap-and-trade program to reduce greenhouse gas emissions 80 percent by 2050. The system would allow pollution credits to be auctioned, with proceeds used to invest in clean energy. Obama says he would re-engage with the UN Framework Convention on Climate Change, the main international forum dedicated to addressing the climate problem. He would also create a Global Energy Forum of the world's largest emitters to focus exclusively on global energy and environmental issues.
FAMILY ISSUES Calling abortion "a human tragedy," McCain has urged the U.S. Supreme Court to overturn the 1973 Roe vs. Wade ruling that legalized it. He supports adoption and with his wife adopted an orphan. He thinks adoption is best for the traditional couple of a man and woman but suggests the question of gay adoption is best left to the states. He opposes a constitutional amendment banning gay marriage. But he argues that federal courts should not overturn state legislation "to preserve the traditional family." And he has promised to appoint federal judges who won't be "legislating from the bench."	Obama often stresses that people who work full time should not live in poverty. He would further raise the minimum wage and index it to inflation, while also significantly increasing the Earned Income Tax Credit. Obama would also seek to require employers to provide seven sick days per year and expand the Family and Medical Leave Act. He supports legalized abortion.
FIREARMS Professing "a sacred duty to protect" the constitutional right to keep and bear arms, McCain also maintains that the government has an obligation to keep firearms out of the hands of criminals. He opposes holding gun manufacturers liable for the commission of crimes and has voted against federal bans on private ownership of assault rifles. He has supported legislation requiring gunmakers to include safety devices such as trigger locks with the weapons. He supports instant criminal background checks for gun buyers, including those at gun shows. But McCain has opposed a waiting period for people buying firearms.	Obama offered a guarded response in June 2008, when the Supreme Court struck down the District of Columbia's prohibition on handguns and sidestepped providing a view on the 32-year-old local gun ban. His carefully worded statement applauded the court for providing "much-needed guidance to local jurisdictions across the country." Obama said he has "always believed that the 2nd Amendment protects the right of individuals to bear arms, but I also identify with the need for crime-ravaged communities to save their children from the violence that plagues our streets through common-sense, effective safety measures." He would re-establish the ban on assault weapons.

Afterword

In Orlando, McCain jokes with employees of Baker Manufacturing after participating in a roundtable discussion with community, business and elected leaders at the company's plant in January 2008.

Credits and sources

CHICAGO TRIBUNE
EDITOR Gerould W. Kern
MANAGING EDITOR, FEATURES James Warren

McCAIN:
The Essential Guide to the Republican Nominee
By Mark Silva

ART DIRECTOR Joan Cairney
PHOTO EDITOR Andrew Johnston
COPY EDITOR Valentina Djeljosevic
RESEARCHER Lelia Boyd Arnheim
IMAGING TECHNICIAN Christine Bruno
PROJECT MANAGERS Chuck Burke, Bill Parker and Susan Zukrow

Introduction: The Warrior
"Faith of My Fathers," by John McCain and Mark Salter, Random House, New York, 1999
"McCain's ancestors owned slaves," by Suzie Parker and Jake Tapper, Salon.com, Feb. 15, 2000
"Bush, McCain in 'death match,'" by Mark Silva, The Miami Herald, Feb. 22, 2000
Interview with Thomas Kean, 9/11 Commission chairman
Speeches by John McCain to Los Angeles World Affairs Council, 2008, and Veterans of Foreign Wars, Kansas City, 1995

1. McCain's Heroes
"Faith of My Fathers," by John McCain and Mark Salter
"McCain's ancestors owned slaves," Salon.com
"USS John S. McCain," U.S. Navy Web site, navysite./de/dd/ddg56.htm
"McCain's Maverick Side: Grandpa Would be Proud," by Jonathan Weisman, The Washington Post, July 22, 2008
"The Nightingale's Song," by Robert Timberg, Simon & Schuster, New York, 1995
"Worth the Fighting For," by John McCain and Mark Salter, Random House, New York, 2002
Yearbook, Episcopal High School, Alexandria, Va., 1954
"The Forrestal Fire," Navy Web site, www.chinfo.navy.mil/navpalib/ships/carriers/histories/cv59-forrestal/forrestal-fire.html
"John McCain, Prisoner of War: A First-Person Account," U.S. News & World Report, May 14, 1973
2. Prisoner of War
"Faith of My Fathers," by John McCain and Mark Salter
"The Nightingale's Song," by Robert Timberg
"John McCain, Prisoner of War," U.S. News & World Report.
Interview with Orson Swindle, former prisoner of war
Speeches by John McCain to Values Voter Summit, Washington, D.C., 2007, and Veterans of Foreign Wars, Kansas City, 1995

3. His Second Life
"Arizona, the early years," by Dan Nowicki and Bill Muller, The Arizona Republic, March 1, 2007
"The Nightingale's Song," by Robert Timberg
"Worth the Fighting For," by John McCain and Mark Salter
"In Search of Cindy McCain," by Holly Bailey, Newsweek, June 30, 2008

4. The Senator
"Arizona, the early years," by Dan Nowicki and Bill Muller, The Arizona Republic, March 1, 2007
"The Keating Five," by Dan Nowicki and Bill Muller, The Arizona Republic, March 1, 2007
"The Senate calls," by Dan Nowicki and Bill Muller, The Arizona Republic, March 1, 2007
"Citizen McCain," by Elizabeth Drew, Simon & Schuster, New York, 2002
"The Almanac of American Politics," by Michael Barone and Richard E. Cohen, National Journal, Washington, D.C., 2008
Letter to President George W. Bush by Sen. John McCain and other members of Congress, Dec. 6, 2001
Interview with Thomas Kean, 9/11 Commission chairman
Interview with John McCain, The Associated Press, Dec. 13, 2004
"Meet the Press," NBC News, June 18, 2005
"Meet the Press," NBC News, Jan. 21, 2007

5. The Senator's Wife
"Worth the Fighting For," by John McCain and Mark Salter
"Arizona, the early years," by Dan Nowicki and Bill Muller, The Arizona Republic
"Cindy McCain: Myth vs. Reality," by Nancy Collins, Harper's Bazaar, July 2007
"A political wife of quiet purpose" by Jill Zuckman, Chicago Tribune, April 15, 2008
"In Search of Cindy McCain," by Holly Bailey, Newsweek, June 30, 2008.
"McCain's broken marriage fractured other ties as well," by Richard A. Serrano and Ralph Vartabedian, Los Angeles Times, July 11, 2008

"Overcoming scandal, moving on," by Dan Nowicki and Bill Muller, The Arizona Republic, March 1, 2007
Appearance by Cindy McCain at Conference for Women, sponsored by First Lady Maria Shriver, Sacramento, Calif., 2007

6. Seeking the White House
"McCain makes candidacy official," by Mark Silva, The Miami Herald, Sept. 28, 1999
"Bush Toughens His Stand Against GOP Rival McCain," by Mark Silva, The Miami Herald, Feb. 11, 2000
"McCain banks on South Carolina in presidential 'crusade,'" by Mark Silva, The Miami Herald, Feb. 6, 2000
"Bush, McCain in 'death match,'" by Mark Silva, The Miami Herald, Feb. 22, 2000
"The 'maverick' runs," by Dan Nowicki and Bill Muller, The Arizona Republic, March 1, 2007
Interview with Mike Murphy, 2000 McCain for President campaign media adviser
"Worth the Fighting For," by John McCain and Mark Salter
John McCain's speech to Republican National Convention, Philadelphia, Aug. 1, 2000

7. The Nominee
The Gallup Poll, March 2-3, 2007
"Late Show with David Letterman," CBS, Feb. 28, 2007
"Saturday Night Live," NBC, Oct. 19, 2002
"Larry King Live," CNN, April 25, 2007
McCain speech to Values Voter Summit, Washington, D.C., October 2007
"For McCain, a Second Try at the White House," by Michael D. Shear, The Washington Post, April 26, 2007
John McCain's commencement address at Liberty University, Lynchburg., Va., 2006
"Meet the Press," NBC News, April 2, 2006
"The 'maverick' runs," by Dan Nowicki and Bill Muller, The Arizona Republic, March 1, 2007
Washington Post-ABC News Poll, Jan. 19, 2007
"Super showdown in amazing race," by Jill Zuckman, Chicago Tribune, Feb. 5, 2008, and other Tribune reports
Republican presidential candidate debate, Ronald Reagan Presidential Library and Museum, Simi Valley, Calif., May 2007
McCain campaign appearance, New Mexico, July 15, 2008
8. McCain, the Man
"Face the Nation," CBS News, Jan. 6, 2008
McCain commencement address, Liberty University, 2006
Yearbook, Episcopal High School, Alexandria, Va., 1954
"The Senate calls," by Dan Nowicki and Bill Muller
Interview with Mike Murphy, 2000 campaign media adviser
Interview with Orson Swindle, former prisoner of war

9. On the Issues
johnmccain.com; barackobama.com; John McCormick; Chicago Tribune archives

PHOTOGRAPHY
Tech. Sgt. Jeffrey Allen, U.S. Air Force: 94-95
Associated Press: 33
John Austad, Chicago Tribune: 22
April Bartholomew, The Morning Call: 114-115
Mark Boster, Los Angeles Times: 8-9, 64-65
Joe Burbank, Orlando Sentinel 10-11, 80-81, 124-125
Joe Cavaretta, South Florida Sun-Sentinel: 88-89
Charles Cherney, Chicago Tribune: 90
Jay L. Clendenin, Los Angeles Times: 6-7, 67, 82-83, 108-109, back cover
Carolyn Cole, Los Angeles Times: 78-79
Kathleen X. Cook, The Morning Call: 14
Nuccio DiNuzzo, Chicago Tribune: 84-85, 86-87
Carol M. Highsmith, Library of Congress: 39
Andrew Innerarity, South Florida Sun-Sentinel: 99, 104-105, 116-117
Chuck Kennedy, McClatchy-Tribune: Cover, 48-49, 50-51, 52-53, 96-97, 112-113
Tim Koors, Phoenix Gazette: 60
Library of Congress: 25, 28-29
North Vietnamese government: 30
Provided by John McCain: 19, 20, 21, 37, 61
Pete Souza, Chicago Tribune:42-43, 44-45, 57, 58-59, 63, 70-71, 73, 74-75, 76, 77, 110
Kuni Takahashi, Chicago Tribune: 46, 100-101, 107
Spencer Weiner, Los Angeles Times: 93
Jill Zuckman, Chicago Tribune: 68-69
U.S. Navy: 26, 34

TYPEFACE
Hoefler Titling and Hoefler Text by Hoefler & Frere-Jones